ADVANCE PRAISE

"*In Defense of Common Life* is a magnificent introduction of Raquel Gutiérrez Aguilar's work to a wider audience. It crystallizes hard-won insights gleaned from four decades of political struggle in Latin America. She interrogates political organization, feminist praxis, and making—the essential social force that capital can never fully contain. To escape capitalism and stultifying definitions of revolution, she illuminates paths to imagine the world anew. Here is a text to wrestle with—a gift in translation."
—**Christina Heatherton**, author of *Arise! Global Radicalism in the Era of the Mexican Revolution*

"Raquel Gutiérrez Aguilar is not only an innovative theorist but also an inspiring activist. This beautifully edited and translated volume charts her extraordinary political trajectory and presents some of her vital contributions to contemporary political and theoretical debates. With this English-language edition, new audiences will be able to benefit from her important work." —**Michael Hardt**, author of *The Subversive Seventies* and coauthor of *Bolivia Beyond the Impasse*

"Few walk the walk that Raquel Gutiérrez Aguilar has, through her involvement in militant struggles such as the Ejército Guerrillero Túpac-Katari and the Water Wars and gas conflicts of Bolivia. *In Defense of Common Life* movingly presents some of the lessons she has learned along the way as 'concisely as possible.' These lessons are about autonomy, the value of lengthy discussion, and the difficult and yet crucial attention that the communal deserves in the fervor of revolutionary struggle. As such, this book is both a handbook for the future and a careful assessment of a complicated past." —**Juliana Spahr**, author of *Du Bois's Telegram*

IN DEFENSE OF COMMON LIFE

Philadelphia, PA
Brooklyn, NY
commonnotions.org

In Defense of Common Life: The Political Thought of Raquel Gutiérrez Aguilar

© Raquel Gutiérrez Aguilar, Brian Whitener
Translated by JD Pluecker

This edition © 2024 Common Notions

ISBN: 978-1-945335-11-2 | eBook ISBN: 978-1-945335-24-2
Library of Congress Number: 2024939163
10 9 8 7 6 5 4 3 2 1

Common Notions
c/o Interference Archive
314 7th St.
Brooklyn, NY 11215

Common Notions
c/o Making Worlds Bookstore
210 S. 45th St.
Philadelphia, PA 19104

www.commonnotions.org
info@commonnotions.org

Discounted bulk quantities of our books are available for organizing, educational, or fundraising purposes. Please contact Common Notions at the address above for more information.

Cover design by Josh MacPhee
Layout design and typesetting by Suba Murugan

IN DEFENSE OF
COMMON
LIFE

The Political Thought of
Raquel Gutiérrez Aguilar

Raquel Gutiérrez Aguilar
Edited by Brian Whitener
Translated by JD Pluecker

CONTENTS

INTRODUCTION

Brian Whitener

Raquel Gutiérrez Aguilar is one of the foremost political thinkers, feminists, and theorists of autonomy in Latin America. Her work, despite its profound insights into Latin American politics, contemporary feminist movements, and theory and practice of producing autonomy, is almost unknown in the United States. This volume has the simple aim of correcting this tremendous oversight and introducing Raquel's thought and political experience to an English-speaking audience, particularly within left circles.

Raquel's work can be distilled into two primary concerns: how autonomy is produced and sustained and how the patriarchal ordering of society can be destroyed. Of course, these two concerns are deeply interconnected and for Raquel they are not merely subjects of theoretical inquiry. One of the strengths of her work is its serious engagement with political realities. In the work contained in this volume, there are no easy celebrations of the commons, but rather careful working throughs of political experience and a profound—moving we might say—desire to overcome the limits of current autonomist struggles.

For many readers, Raquel's work will also present a different vision of struggles over the last decades in Latin America. Instead of a glorification of progressive governments, such as those of Evo Morales in Bolivia or Luiz Inácio Lula da Silva in Brazil, to say nothing of Andrés Manuel López Obrador in Mexico, Raquel is a resolute representative of the "critical left" perspective which has yet to receive much attention in the United States and other English-speaking areas. This position is fiercely critical of states, even so-called "progressive" ones. The last three decades have been marked—argues Raquel—by an upsurge of movements seeking to reappropriate social wealth and its means of reproduction from states and capital. These movements have been, frustratingly at times, tragically at others, co-opted back into state and capitalist circuits and have been unable to move beyond what Raquel calls a "capacity for social veto" and to generate the conditions for the reproduction of a different society. In short, the cycle of progressive governments since 2001 in Latin America are *a problem*, not a solution. As readers will see, much of Raquel's work has been dedicated to thinking about how to move beyond this impasse of movements sustaining their power, and it is here that her work offers a significant contribution to current conversations on commoning.

Raquel was born in Mexico and came of age politically in the early 1980s, when armed struggle and seizure of the state apparatus were still the dominant revolutionary strategy. This was the moment of the great Central American revolutionary struggles, when the legacy of the Cuban revolution was given new life and meaning in El Salvador, Nicaragua, and Guatemala. Raquel's first political experiences, as she details in the interview contained in the volume, were in the revolutionary armed groups of El Salvador, which were fighting to overthrow the military junta that had seized power in 1972. Her experiences of the centralism of these movements, and their patriarchal ordering, is one root of Raquel's lifelong work of understanding how autonomy can be built and sustained without the structures of the state and capitalism.

After a brief sojourn in Mexico, Raquel moved to Bolivia, where she became involved in the *Ejército Guerrillero Túpac Katari* [Túpac Katari Guerilla Army] or EGTK, an armed, heavily Aymara resistance movement. The EGTK was composed of three sectors: Aymara Indigenous groups based in the Bolivian Highlands, miners and other radicalized workers, and students and other urban militants of which Raquel formed a part. The EGTK departed from the fully centralized, hierarchical model of other armed groups and by the late 1980s they were a potent political force in Bolivia. Long histories of struggle and practices of discussion and assembly—as Raquel notes—informed their organizing structures but their success, as well as their dramatic actions, put them squarely in the crosshairs of state repression. By 1992, their key leaders were arrested and in prison. Raquel was among them, and she spent five years being held without charges in a Bolivian women's prison.

Like many great revolutionary intellectuals before her, Raquel used prison to study and reflect, and she produced a balance sheet of contemporary struggles and her organizing up to that point. Her first book *¡A desordenar! [Disrupt!]* demonstrates her profound antipathy for hierarchy and calls for a turn from armed struggle to "communitarian self-determination." It also records her experience, while in prison, of watching the Zapatista revolution, with its emphasis on autonomy and critique of the aim of taking state power, unfold in her home country of Mexico and the resonances between that Indigenous struggle and form of organizing with her own experiences in Bolivia.

First published in 1995, *¡A desordenar!* also registers the deep imprint and significance for Raquel—both for her political thought and future organizing—of being held in a *women's* prison. A series of critical events, including organizing a hunger strike and rebellion against prison conditions, as well as working with outside organizers to free EGTK members and herself, opened onto the second great theme of her work: patriarchy. *Desandar el laberinto* [*Retracing the Labyrinth*], published just a few years later, centers the role of women in the production of concrete social wealth—which has become an important thread through her most recent work—and offers a trenchant critique of liberal feminism and the politics of formalistic, legal equality.

Raquel's organizing eventually led to her release along with the rest of her EGTK comrades. Granted her freedom, Raquel remained in Bolivia and lived one of the first open rebellions in Latin America against neoliberalism, the Bolivian Water War, a months-long uprising against the privatization of water. During this time, Raquel threw herself into organizing once again working with the Coordinadora del agua, fighting for the creation of an autonomous political force to manage water in the Cochibamba region of La Paz.

Once again facing state repression, Raquel returned to Mexico and wrote a dissertation reflecting on the lessons of the Bolivian Water and Gas Wars for autonomous politics. In this work, *Los ritmos del Pachakuti* (published in English in 2014 as *Rhythms of the Pachakuti*), Raquel examines the possibilities and limits of autonomous politics in the sequence of the water and gas wars, and she develops concepts to explain those limits but also to help autonomous militants overcome them. Ideas such as "the social capacity to veto," "community interweavings," and "the communitarian-popular horizon," have become foundational for her current work on autonomist, communitarian, and feminist struggle in the present.

The energy of the Bolivian uprising was, sadly, diverted into yet another state-centric solution: the MAS party and the election of Evo Morales. As Raquel has detailed in her work, in the decades since the Zapatista uprising, this is a story that has played out again and again across Latin America: popular, autonomist energies coming from uprisings, rebellions, and social movements are channeled back into state and capitalist structures. Raquel has been at the forefront of articulating this "critical left" position emerging from feminist, Indigenous, student and autonomist movements. Too often in the United States and North Atlantic this critical perspective has been drowned out by, sometimes well-intentioned, celebrations of "left parties" seizing power—which is another motivation in presenting Raquel's work to a broad, English-speaking audience.

Her interventions over the last decade anticipated and have centered the massive feminist uprising which has exploded since 2015 across Latin America. In this emerging body of work, Raquel returns to her earlier work on patriarchy, how it structures the political forms of autonomous organizing, and how the present feminist movement could both move beyond this impasse and destroy the patriarchal social relations which sustain it.

This book opens with an interview conducted with Raquel via email in the summer of 2023. In a wide-ranging discussion, we walk through her history within political groups such as the EGTK and her theoretical endeavors. The interview aims to present a broad, yet accessible, overview of some of the central preoccupations of Raquel's organizing and writing. Following this interview are translations of two essays which exemplify Raquel's theoretical concerns and which elaborate some of the conceptual vocabulary that she has developed.

The first essay, "Beyond the 'Capacity to Veto,'" demonstrates three of Raquel's principal interventions. The first focuses our attention on the production of social wealth that occurs constantly all around us. Much of this takes place through capitalist and state circuits, but there is some that does not. Raquel's question is: how can we collectively reappropriate (what she calls) "social flows of making"? The second involves her reading of recent Latin American history as an upsurge of forces searching and pressing for the reappropriation of social wealth. Her reading of—what has become known in English as—the "progressive cycle" or the "Pink Tide" governments (think Evo, Lula, etc.) is that these were ways of channeling this energy back into the state and capital. We can see how Raquel is not merely doing political theory but works concretely out of an intimate knowledge of the impasses of Latin American movements. Finally, in this essay—and its helpful table towards the conclusion— Raquel sketches, picking up from the long histories of Indigenous autonomy in the region, how the mechanisms for the collective reappropriation of social wealth differ from those of the liberal/democratic state.

The second essay, "Producing the Common," presents some of the theoretical results of Raquel's work in the research group *Entramados comunitarios y formas de lo político* [Community Weavings and Forms of the Political] that she helps lead at the Universidad Autónoma de Puebla. At the center of this newly translated work is the term "reproduction" and the insight that struggles for the common almost always are organized around a defense of the reproduction of life. This centering of reproduction, as opposed to the more visible dynamics of capital accumulation, Raquel calls a "Copernican revolution" for her thought. The essay also presents three key insights derived from the collective work she's undertaken in the Entramados group. The first is a culmination of Raquel's long engagement with and participation in Indigenous struggles: that the communitarian is not necessarily Indigenous and indigeneity is not necessarily communal. As Raquel writes elsewhere, Indigenous traditions in Latin America are an incredibly rich source for understanding how collective social wealth is produced and maintained over time, but not all Indigenous communities are examples of this, nor is the ability to produce collective wealth confined to them. The second insight is that the communal is not something static, something found inert in the world, but rather that it is a relation, something that must be produced. And finally, that the production of a common(s), or the conditions necessary for a common life, requires the overcoming and moving beyond the separations imposed through dispossession and the patriarchal exploitation of capital.

We hope these texts hold for readers as much promise for deepening practices of autonomous politics as they did for us, and we hope they contribute to the ongoing intensification of connections and dialogues across languages and political traditions in this hemisphere. If you are interested in reading more of Raquel's work beyond this volume, the following texts are a few starting points in English and Spanish.

ENGLISH

"Beyond the Arithmetic of Gender Equality," *Ojalá,* September 30, 2023, https://www.ojala.mx/en/ojala-en/beyond-the-arithmetic-of-gender-equality.

"Social Reproduction, Rebellion and the Problem of the State," *Ojalá,* June 9, 2023, https://www.ojala.mx/en/ojala-en/reproduction-rebellion-and-the-problem-of-the-state.

"Amplifying feminist struggle in the wake of March 8," trans. María José López, *Ojalá*, March 17, 2023, https://www.ojala.mx/en/ojala-en/amplifying-feminist-struggle-in-the-wake-of-march-8.

"Letters to My Younger Sisters," trans. Dawn Marie Paley and Liz Mason-Deese, *Ill Will*, February 8, 2023, https://illwill.com/letters-to-my-younger-sisters.

Rhythms of the Pachakuti: Indigenous Uprising and State Power in Bolivia, trans. Stacey Alba D. Skar (Durham: Duke University Press, 2014).

SPANISH

¡A desordenar! Por una historia abierta de la lucha social (México: Pez en el árbol, 2014).

Desandar el laberinto. Introspección en la feminidad contemporánea (México: Pez en el árbol, 2010).

Horizonte comunitario-popular. Antagonismo y producción de lo común en América Latina (México: Benemérita Universidad Autónoma de Puebla, 2015).

1 | "THERE IS NO POLITICAL AUTONOMY WITHOUT MATERIAL AUTONOMY": AN INTERVIEW WITH RAQUEL GUTIÉRREZ AGUILAR

This interview was conducted via email in Summer 2023.

Brian Whitener: Your first political experiences took place in the context of the Sandinista struggle of the 1980s. How did these experiences shape you? What role did they play in the longer arc of your life in politics?

Raquel Gutiérrez Aguilar: Perhaps I should begin by talking a bit about the larger context of the victory of the Sandinista revolution. On July 19, 1979, Sandinista forces were able to take Managua. [President Anastasio] Somoza departed, his regime fell, and the Sandinistas began to rebuild the government. I didn't participate at all in those events. I was very young, and I didn't understand much, though everything happening in El Salvador was a source of a lot of hope, at least for us in Mexico.

1981 saw the beginning of my involvement in these experiences of revolutionary struggle—which were codified through the language of "national liberation." As people said at the time, "Central America is burning," and the civil wars for liberation in Guatemala and El Salvador were intensifying. Those were years when many refugees, including many Central Americans, were arriving in Mexico. I enrolled at the National Autonomous University of Mexico (UNAM) at the end of 1980, and the environment I encountered was infused with solidarity around those two historic struggles.

That's how I began to gradually be involved in the Central American struggles taking place at the time. This played an important role in my subsequent political work and education.

Specifically, I developed deeper connections with what was happening in El Salvador. I learned a lot by participating in outreach work, propaganda, education, support for refugees, etc. There were rigidly codified ways of understanding the events of the time, and I learned to draw distinctions between them.

In particular, it was crucial to distinguish between the different political strategies being deployed in this moment. For example, to be able understand the differences between the various organizations that composed the Salvadoran FMLN (Farabundo Martí National Liberation Front) or the Guatemalan URNG (Guatemalan National Revolutionary Unity), I was learning to identify certain features and elements, or rather, I was learning to ask certain questions: Who were the "subjects of the revolution"? What programs were they pushing? And what were the politics of alliance they practiced?

This way of understanding organizations and political events was woven into an overarching heroic narrative, and the goal to be achieved was very clear: taking political power. To comprehend what was happening, one needed to identify the subjects of the struggle, the programs being pushed, and the alliances formed.

Throughout 1982, the organizational structures sustaining the war in El Salvador began to enter into crisis. Specifically, during an intense and virulent repression that was both targeted and widespread, one of the organizations that composed the FMLN, the *Fuerzas Populares de Liberación* [Popular Liberation Forces], or FPL by its acronym in Spanish, expressed its opposition to certain decisions made by the other organizations within the FMLN, due to its issues with alliance politics and the political program. The FPL—the organization I was working with—was shaken by a bitter and traumatic process of internal division that ended with the deaths of its two main leaders. In fact, it was even more extreme than that: one leader had ordered the assassination of the other, and then he took his own life. This is a terrible episode in the history of revolutionary struggle in Latin America. The disagreements that led to that fatal outcome were related to the conduct of the ongoing war, and, it must be repeated, occurred at a time of brutal repression. And, for the same reason, they were tied to fundamental political issues.

On the one hand, my experience of these events and the discussions surrounding them was quite intense, and it was repeatedly marked by profound levels of misunderstanding due to the secrecy with which even the most fundamental political discussions were conducted within a vertical, centralized, and compartmentalized organizational structure. The documents that circulated among the organization's members—and I was a member at the time—and militants were secret and distributed in a compartmentalized way.

Because of this, I could never get a sufficiently complete idea about what was happening and what was at stake in each of the larger political debates. This was even though what was called "democratic centralism"—the name of the classic organizing principle we used—presupposed the need for a broad political debate prior to centralization in leadership.

Though I didn't have these words at the time, and I only found them later, I'd say that to me it seemed strange that militants were not invited to participate in the production of political decisions; rather, they were positioned as individuals who had to follow decisions made by central leadership. What's more, there was hardly ever a commonly shared vision guiding those decisions.

In a book I wrote long ago called ¡A desordenar! [Disrupt!], I reflected on what the FMLN's so-called "programmatic change" meant, as it transitioned from advocating for the creation of a "revolutionary democratic government" to a "government of broad participation."

In January 1984, amid all these events and at the age of twenty-one, I made my way to El Salvador. I was immediately detained at a clandestine meeting of the Revolutionary Trade Union Federation, which was raided by the army and the police. I had a very difficult time in the National Police headquarters, and a few days later, I was deported to Mexico.

This experience affected me deeply, as I came to understand it over time by developing my own critique of the structural authoritarianism of vertical and centralized organizational forms. The critique of these types of organizational principles became a throughline in all my subsequent experiences.

BW: You touched on something that's always caught my attention about your political organizing: a disagreement with or perhaps even a hatred of hierarchy, which has been present since your earliest political experiences.

I'd like to revisit your discussion of democratic centralism in ¡A desordenar! In this book, you write, "[B]ut it was this discussion [about democratic centralism] that marked me forever and became, over time, one of my deepest convictions. We had to organize, of course, but not in the bureaucratic centralist manner I had experienced in Central America. Instead, we had to promote what I consider a true democratic centralism: everything needed to be up for debate, structures needed to facilitate actions rather than impede them, and transparency and plain-spoken clarity had to be our behavioral norms. In short, we had to emphasize democracy more than centralism." After your experiences in El Salvador, you went to Bolivia and participated in the creation of the *Ejército Guerrillero Tupac-Katari* [Tupac-Katari Guerrilla Army] (known as EGTK by its Spanish acronym), which was a mixed group of Aymara and non-Aymara militants attempting to offer, in my interpretation, a solution to these problems of militarism and centralism in the formation of a strategy for armed struggle. How did the approach of the EGTK emerge? How did they conceive of and implement a political approach combining Aymara communal forms and Marxist traditions? And how did your involvement with the EGTK shift your own perspective about "a real democratic centralism" or what today is often called "autonomy"?

RG: You're asking a few different questions here. Perhaps it would be best to address them one by one.

The experience of the EGTK emerged out of the convergence of very different groups that grew closer together over time. On the one hand, there was a group of Aymara compañeros and compañeras who had acquired extensive political experience in struggles against the harshest dictatorships in Bolivia during the 1970s and early '80s; the most experienced among them were ten to fifteen years older than us, "the urbanites." Those compañeros had participated in the resistance against the military coups; they had gained experience through the road blockades of 1979 and had participated in an electoral struggle through a legal political organization.

As far as us, "we" were also a quite complex grouping of individuals: some of us were former students and "urban-ites" working full-time on political organizing, along with another set of compañeros—primarily men—who were miners or factory workers. When we first came up with our name, prior to becoming the EGTK, we called ourselves the *Ofensiva Roja* [Red Offensive]. We all shared that name, but different groupings also added on different "last names." So the section of the group composed of urbanites and work-ers signed its documents as "Ofensiva Roja, Miners' Cells." The compañeros from the rural areas who were of Aymara origin signed off as "Ofensiva Roja of the Tupac-Katari Ayllus." This way of relating between groups was productive because it was based on the composition of several parts— or of autonomous segments, as I have thought of them for a long time. It is a very useful technique, and there is much wisdom in it: it makes coordination and proximity visible, while still leaving room for difference. Felipe Quispe had a saying he would use to explain why there were "two" Ofensivas Rojas: "The condor flies with both wings." So we had shared meetings and we would discuss and approve documents together, but at the same time each segment was autonomous unto itself and had its own documents, books, and even its own newspaper. Each one had its own voice. That's why we were never required to "fuse together" into one single position. The unification was practical: we were doing the same things, even though each would emphasize different aspects of what was taking place.

In those early years of the convergence between these groups, I was heavily involved in the work of what was called "press and propaganda," although I think it was more than that, because it involved not only technical aspects like editing, printing, distributing, etc.; rather, I would often write things with my compañeros alongside me, telling me what they wanted their texts to say, especially when there were documents written in Spanish. We would discuss nuances, different ways of expressing the same ideas, and sometimes also content.

Across several years, we had a lot of informal conversations and many meetings, since there were always several compañeros working to produce materials at the "press and propaganda" office. Later, those exchanges extended into large-scale gatherings that were much more formal. However, I think that much of the work of building connections, listening, and understanding others' points of view actually took place informally in those many previous conversations. That's how we operated from the end of 1985 until around 1990. We also conducted many educational activities on various topics, politics, technical skills, etc.

The key to bringing together all these differing organizational forms was that the majority of the compañeros brought with them a very deep practice of deliberation and assembly. The Aymara compañeros would use their own unhurried methods of discussion and decision-making, and the miners and factory workers would also bring their profound experiences with union organizing; they also knew how to debate and how to make collective decisions since that was the practice in their grassroots labor organizations.

The problem that emerged a little later, around 1991, was that, first, we were increasing in scale—the organization had grown significantly—and second, the need to work clandestinely had intensified, and security measures had become stricter. This started to complicate our organizing methods, and it demanded a lot from our leadership group, who had to work hard to disseminate information to the entire organization. In any case, what I learned was that as long as political discussions among all members of the organization remained open and only specific issues related to the security of militants and resources were compartmentalized, things worked quite well.

What didn't work as well in the long run was how each person came to understand their experience in the EGTK and what they did with it. A few years after getting out of prison, Felipe Quispe and the Aymara compañeros led a significant portion of the major mobilizations that were responsible for restraining neoliberalism in Bolivia, and they also founded a registered political party. The García Linera brothers moved toward the MAS (Movement for Socialism) and ended up in conflict with Quispe and some of his compañeros. As for me, I continued my work with public discussions and producing texts offering critical analysis, for example in *Comuna*, and by putting into practice what I had learned during the Water War in Cochabamba. Later, I came back to Mexico, soon after the Zapatista March of the Color of the Earth (February 24–March 28, 2001).

At that time, one thing I hadn't realized was just how detrimental *caudillismo*[1] in politics could be. I couldn't envision how some individuals—especially the García Linera brothers—would attempt to take advantage of the efforts made by everyone else. For many years, we had engaged in a practice of democratic, autonomous politics that was occasionally centralized, but what I perceived later was a struggle between caudillos to seize the power generated collectively for their own benefit.

BW: You were imprisoned between 1992 and 1997. In *¡A desordenar!*, you dedicate a chapter to your experience in prison. You were fighting both from inside the prison to

---

[1] *Caudillismo* is a political structure where a single person monopolizes political, social, and economic power and uses clientelist relations to structure and maintain power.—Ed.

get your freedom and the freedom of your compañerxs, and as part of a political grouping that included participants from *Mujeres Creando* [Women Creating]. Beyond this, you were doing political work inside the prison, organizing with other prisoners to improve their lives inside and to put an end to certain practices of the prison's administration.

Like many other former political prisoners, it seems that while in prison you experienced moments that were both horrifying and uplifting. In *¡A desordenar!* you write, "Once in prison, one of the most intense and enlightening human actions I have experienced was the uprising in February 1993. That event was undoubtedly an excellent example of self-assertion, resistance, and defense of individual sovereignty, and later, collective sovereignty."[2] How were you impacted by this experience of being a prisoner, and specifically, a prisoner in an institution designated for women? Why was the uprising an "experience of extreme self-assertion and uncompromising defense of a sovereign decision," and how did it shape your political and intellectual development?

RG: In prison, once I had recovered from the initial shock of my arrest and understood the new outlines of my daily life and the kinds of problems I would face, I did the same thing I had done for the past ten years: I made an effort to understand the problems we shared, engaged in conversations with my compañeras, and attempted to find ways to organize ourselves to collectively present our grievances. The prison where I was held was not a maximum-security facility with prisoners divided into fully individualized cells; in fact, it was the complete opposite: the population fluctuated between 230–250 women, with pretrial detain-

---

[2] Raquel Gutiérrez Aguilar, *¡A desordenar! Por una historia abierta de la lucha social* (México: Pez en el árbol, 2014), 85.

ees mixed with those serving sentences. Children could live with their mothers up to the age of five years, despite the lack of infrastructure and very small amount of space. The main problem of everyday life was overcrowding, not loneliness or the strict rules of the prison regime. I spent five years in these conditions.

The main problem we all faced was not so much the prison regime—which sometimes could become more or less rigid—but rather the negligence and ineffectiveness of the judges and, in general, the officials within the judicial system. They simply didn't do their jobs, and cases and proceedings piled up while people remained in prison for years with no legal developments and, of course, no sentencing. The poorest individuals found themselves in this situation because they did not have enough resources to pay to move their legal proceedings forward or to achieve favorable outcomes.

According to the prison classification system, there were three groups of female detainees: common prisoners, those arrested under anti-drug laws—who faced special, harsher punishment under Law 1008—and the third group, which included us, the political prisoners. Each group faced different problems in terms of the legal process, and within the prison, the way the police maintained order was, in part, by pitting different groups against each other.

The first prison uprising I experienced took place in February 1993, ten months after my arrival in April 1992. By then, I was already familiar with the dynamics of the facility, its mechanisms of control, and how the police operated. I had also gotten to know my fellow prisoners, and we had started to gather information to be able to discuss our common problems. Common prisoners charged with economic crimes faced, among other things, issues related to "civil damages." This meant that in addition to their prison sentences—which were typically around five years for offenses such as fraud, theft, etc.—they had to be able to compensate their victims financially for the "damage" they had caused. This was absolutely impossible, and there were several women who had completed their sentences but could not leave the prison due to their inability to pay the compensation. In practical terms, this was "life imprisonment for debt" because these women could not leave until they'd paid off their debts. There was even one woman who had died in prison, despite having completed her sentence.

The women detained under the anti-drug law, Law 1008, they suffered severe mistreatment upon arrest, their due process rights were violated, and they were unable to access so-called "good-time benefits," so almost all of them would spend many years in prison.

Typically, these detainees were drug users who became involved in small-scale drug sales, while others were women who had worked as cooks or laundry workers in the drug production camps. Finally, there was a small group of women who were involved in large-scale drug sales or who were partners of men involved in large-scale drug production or sales. As for us, the political prisoners who the judicial system did not recognize as such, we faced slow and complicated legal processes, and we would likely receive very long sentences. That was the landscape.

The way to "do politics" in prison was to gather information about the situation of each group through numerous detailed conversations with fellow prisoners. We would then engage in lengthy discussions to come up with commonly held political goals. That's how we began to present our grievances to the judicial authorities, systematically and collectively. Over time, we achieved quite a lot, including the modification of certain articles of the penal code and of legal proceedings.

All this work ran counter to the insidious police practice of organizing and promoting distrust among the prisoners, in order to turn us against one another. I have spoken about the February 1993 uprising as an experience of collective affirmation, because it generated a strong collective capacity—among the female prisoners—to challenge the decision to put a fellow prisoner and myself into solitary confinement, because we were demanding the right to see our husbands, who were also imprisoned.

What our fellow prisoners said during the uprising was, "If they do this to them now, they will do it to us tomorrow." There was a capacity here for mutual recognition and also, we might say, to "achieve justice," or rather, to dispute the terms of what was actually just: it was not right to isolate us, because we had the right to demand what we needed, and thus, they simply rioted and refused to let us be punished. That experience was very powerful for me: how my fellow prisoners were able to subvert this ploy by the police and to confront them directly, to calculate the risks, and to establish a dynamic of simultaneous advance and retreat as needed. It was the collective wisdom of women put into action at a specific moment. It was a strategy and a practice that affirmed our own power, a struggle revolving around collective self-defense.

It was very different from what I had seen previously. With the words and knowledge I have now, I would say that what I experienced was the way women were able to engage in struggle in a nonpatriarchal way. At that time, I did not have enough language to describe what I was experiencing, despite having wonderful interlocutors in my compañeras from Mujeres Creando. What I was living contrasted sharply from my previous experiences, and I realized that there was a huge difference that I was not able to express clearly. In part, that's why I began to write *¡A desordenar!* In addition, the 1994 Zapatista uprising drove me to write, as we were learning about their arguments and the demands they were making. I was interested in contrasting my previous experiences with the ideas that were emerging from Chiapas in order to comprehend what I was going through at the time.

Finally, I was interested in engaging in a debate about our own political practice as a defensive strategy, particularly how we understood so-called "revolutionary violence." We needed to take apart, to the greatest extent possible, the imposing, rigid legal apparatus that distinguished between guilt and innocence. The Zapatistas had also done that— and it impressed me greatly—when they responded to a government offer of amnesty by asking, "Who should be asking for forgiveness, and who can actually grant it?" I believe this occurred in 1995.

BW: In 2001, after seventeen years in Bolivia, you returned to Mexico, but not before participating in the early uprisings of *La Guerra del agua* [Water War]. You wrote an entire book, *Los ritmos del Pachakuti* [*The Rhythms of Pachakuti*], about Indigenous struggles in Bolivia between 2000 and 2005. In this book, you develop a set of concepts like "the capacity to veto" and "the communitarian-popular perspective" to help us think about autonomist politics. What was your activism like during that time? What were the main tensions or political issues you wanted to address in this book [*Los ritmos*]? I feel like ideas like the capacity to veto and the communitarian-popular perspective were your primary lessons from this stage of struggle. How do you explain the importance of these ideas for your thinking and political action, and how do they connect with your ideas about how we can produce autonomy?

RG: Yes, the groundwork for the Cochabamba Water War was laid at the end of 1999 and then it unfolded between January and April 2000. At that time, with the diverse compañerxs who made up the *Coordinadora de Defensa del Agua* *y de la Vida* [Coordinating Group for the Defense of Water and Life], I was able to put into practice, in a very intuitive way, everything I had learned in the previous years about the articulation of differences and the importance of clear, mass-based actions that affirmed collective power. On the one hand, these actions reorganized public political discussion, and then additionally they sparked intense processes of deliberation about potential paths forward. In a way, I had learned that strategy does not precede action, rather it orients and channels it, without limiting it.

As struggles unfold, they are constantly confronted with new and wider dilemmas that emerge out of what is opened up and becomes possible through the very act of struggle. I had learned this from previous experiences, particularly during the prison riots and while organizing the actions that led to us being released from prison. I outline this process in the second of my "Letters to My Younger Sisters."[3]

In my view, what happens when a struggle is unfolding—often in a contradictory way and typically under great pressure—is that many possibilities are opened. Possibilities are opened up by a vigorous "No" or a cry of *¡Basta!* [Enough!]. That is, when the social capacity for veto is exercised to reject projects that are not beneficial for society or that aggressively attack society itself or the people who fight back (such as privatizing the water in a city or sentencing people to solitary confinement in prison).

When a struggle unfolds and a limit is established, what is exercised is a collective capacity to veto whatever is being imposed on society. That is the moment when an opening is created, and it must be used. This is why it is critical to have a clear horizon for the struggle, in regard

---

[3] Raquel's first "Letter to My Younger Sisters" has been published in translation by *Ill Will*, https://illwill.com/letters-to-my-younger-sisters.—Ed.

to what one intends to achieve in coordination with those engaged in struggle. Thus, the importance of knowing where the movement wants to arrive or "what we want to see happen," because the subsequent steps are constantly adjusted according to the amount of power generated and what is illuminated by the agreed upon horizon.

This is how I understand the politics of autonomy. However, for the capacity to veto to develop, what is needed are diverse organizational forces and deliberative capacities to produce shared positions, and, of course, material resources to sustain the struggles. If all of this is required, then there is a lot of work to be done and issues to confront. There are many things to do, and what is quite challenging is for that broad set of activities and achievements to build up and to mutually reinforce shared capacities. In other words, how can the autonomy of each group or sector of a struggle not turn into autarky for each of them, and how can they avoid—at least at first—engaging in competitive relationships? Avoiding that, how can they get on the same wavelength to be able to produce a self-reinforcing loop in each area of the struggle based on a shared idea of reciprocal cooperation?

I learned all of this clearly during the Water War, although I already had other, smaller experiences that allowed me to orient myself within the dynamics that are triggered when powerful moments of struggle are unleashed. These are issues that one first learns in practice. Reflecting subsequently on all of this has been very important to me, and when I returned to Mexico, I had enough time to do so because I had a grant to write *Los ritmos del Pachakuti*. I finished writing the book in 2008, that is, two years into Evo Morales' first presidential administration, as the process of Constituent Assemblies in Bolivia was already underway. At that time, I didn't know how to present an argument about the strategy of going "beyond" the capacity to veto.

Nonetheless, it was already clear that the reconstruction of a state, even a "plurinational" one, could not be the goal of a transformative politics with a communitarian-popular horizon. Back then, I didn't know how to clearly frame this difference, beyond criticizing what the MAS [Movement for Socialism] was doing. However, I managed to out-line some pieces of documented contradictions, especially between the collective subversion of what exists—i.e., the desire to alter the way certain activities are organized, for example, in the management of the municipal water com-pany—and a state-centric way of doing politics.

Now, many years later, I use the expression—proposed by Diego Castro—that the "capacity to veto" also requires cultivating the shared will to achieve a general re-equilib-rium in regard to a specific problem. Thinking about and debating the terms—in a broad sense—of the possible or desirable re-equilibrium on some specific, or even every specific, issue that affects those who are struggling and sus-taining life is part of the work of refining what is meant by the communitarian-popular horizon.

This is because one issue to avoid is the translation of the language of struggles into state formulations that truncate, simplify, and, above all, fix and entrench. They hinder or limit the continuity of the creative flows of struggles.

Additionally, when I arrived back in Mexico, I began to understand another way of thinking about autonomy, especially after 2003 when the Zapatistas began to focus on consolidating their self-governing structures in the Caracoles. The construction of structures of self-governance has been a very powerful experience, and yet what I per-ceived was that they had set aside the struggle against the state's push to privatize, which was ongoing at that time.

Upon arriving in Mexico, I became involved in the struggle against privatization, specifically in the Mexican electricity industry. This struggle also included efforts to democratize the electrical workers' union. I participated in that movement for several years and noticed how stark the contradictions were in Mexico between state-centric and autonomous politics. As I became more acquainted with the struggles in Mexico, I developed an argument about a possible popular-communitarian horizon. The inversion of terms—from communitarian-popular to popular-communitarian—is not a superficial change; rather, what necessitates this shift is the scope of the state relationship, its depth and density, as well as the existence or absence of community capacities for self-governance in a broad-based manner. This is what I was learning in Mexico.

BW: There is a section of *Los ritmos* that I find quite crucial, in which you write about the limitations of movements during the Water War and the Gas War: "Rural and urban Aymaras, coca growers, irrigators, and water users from different parts of Bolivia, men and women organized in their various aggregative bodies—communities, unions, committees, etc.—were able to build considerable strength at a local level, giving rise to a kind of tensely-held, actual autonomous interregnum that, nonetheless, failed to conceptualize itself as an ongoing emancipation strategy."[4] I have always thought of your following book, *Horizonte comunitario-popular* [*Communitarian-Popular Horizon*], as an attempt to respond to this deficiency and provide us with a horizon or a world of concepts within which autonomy can be seen as a real strategy for emancipation. In the essays collected in *Horizonte*, we find fruitful concepts such as the "communitarian weaving," "politics in the feminine,"

---

[4] Raquel Gutiérrez Aguilar, *Los ritmos del Pachakuti. Movilización y levantamiento indígena-popular en Bolivia (2000–2005)* (Buenos Aires: Tinta Limón/Universidad Internacional de Andalucía, 2008), 127.

and "reappropriation of common wealth." How did this book come about, and how do the concepts you develop, such as communitarian weaving, politics in the feminine, and the appropriation of common wealth, respond to the challenges that autonomous movements face or faced?

RG: Yes, what you are saying is correct. In *Los ritmos*, I note something that a former compañero, Eugenio Rojas, who was the mayor of Achacachi at the time, told me: "We have known how to destroy institutions but not how to build institutions." He said this with a good deal of bitterness, as he felt trapped in the official institutionality of the Achacachi Municipality. He would often express a message commonly heard from public officeholders within various progressive reform processes: the constant lament or complaint about what "cannot be done" due to the established order—both legal and procedural—voiced alongside their good intentions. It is that discourse that asks you to judge them by what they say and not by what they do.

That formulation kept swirling in my mind because what I noticed was that, except during very heightened moments of confrontation, what hadn't been achieved was the recognition of the organizations themselves or the sustained articulations of struggle as structures of self-governance, that is, as institutions capable of exercising self-governance. In Bolivia, there was so much confusion during the rebellion, especially between 2004 and 2005, regarding the importance of "taking over" the government through electoral means. Moreover, from the government's side, the main task was reorganizing the state instead of continuing to dismantle its power and control, which was what the struggles had already achieved.

When I started working at the University of Puebla and had more time for reflection and to learn about other processes—like in Argentina or Venezuela—I began to encounter similar situations. Contradictions between social capacities for struggle and an internal lack of awareness of the ability to self-govern attained at certain moments in time. This became a central object of my reflection in *Horizonte comunitario-popular*. . . . And indeed, the most challenging problem is the reappropriation of social wealth that goes beyond traditional legal forms, that is, beyond the establishment of state property.

In Bolivia, as well as in other countries, the struggle for social wealth had been intense, and it opened up possible paths that were ultimately blocked by other positions that offered "state-centric" solutions. Hence the importance of Diego Castro's formulation that I mentioned earlier, related to the "desire for general re-equilibrium" as a core aspect to cultivate during social struggles focused on specific issues that broaden the possibilities of disrupting the established order. That is the direction my work took for a few years, until 2017.

BW: The idea of wealth and control of wealth shows up in your second book, *Desandar el laberinto* [*Retracing the Labyrinth*], which emerged from a sustained engagement with feminism. In this book, you theorize a distinction between a "universe of abstract wealth and a universe of concrete wealth that is gradually abstracted."[5] The connections between the (re)production of wealth and gender are woven throughout your work. In your more recent texts, concepts such as interdependence, collective labor, and the production of the common emerge, along with a vision of communitarian or autonomous struggles that "almost always organize and unfold around collective efforts to defend the material and symbolic conditions necessary for

---

[5] Raquel Gutiérrez Aguilar, *Desandar el laberinto. Introspección en la feminidad contemporánea* (México: Pez en el árbol, 2010), 113.

guaranteeing the reproduction of common life." At the same time, you have participated as a theorist and activist in the large feminist mobilizations that have unfolded across the continent since 2015. For you, how do these lines of thought and experience intersect, that is, gender and the common? Today, how do you view the movements—both communal and feminist—and their possibilities, limitations, and challenges? Do you believe we have reached a moment when autonomy is perceived as a true path to emancipation?

RG: We have reached the most challenging questions, because they are the ones that are still unresolved for me, and you're right, they have accompanied me throughout my life, or at least for the past twenty-five years. In the women's prison, my approach to feminism was theoretical due to the dialogue and friendship I developed with Mujeres Creando, but it was also very strong in terms of lived experience. Perhaps this is what has taken me the longest time to process.

During that time, I learned two things. The issue of "subjects of struggle" was quite ambiguous because such "subjects" were never a given, they were neither determined by identity markers nor did they exist prior to the struggles. Those who struggle find their composition by opening and sustaining the processes of struggle that constitute them as subjects in motion. Thus, it has always been important to me to concentrate on this relationship of "being part of." How does one become part of a collective or larger body that brings people together, containing you but without determining you? And, now thinking in collective terms, how does one group or body find its composition with another or multiple others? How is that gradual unification sustained and amplified? As all of this is quite fluid, where are the dangers that one part might "appropriate" everyone else's work and efforts?

As I was part of the group of women prisoners in La Paz for several years, I witnessed how this issue of the formation of subjects in and for struggle unfolded among them, with all their immense strength and creativity. There were similarities in this way of constellating capacities for struggle with what I had learned years earlier during the organization of the EGTK [Guerrilla Army of the Poor]. However, it wasn't exactly the same. There were some aspects of women's struggles that caught my attention, which I experienced as different, although I didn't have the language to express, specify, and differentiate them.

In *Desandar el laberinto* [*Retracing the Labyrinth*], I began to explore that language, and I did so by mixing two traditions: the concrete and struggle-oriented feminism that advocates for the use of the first person, reflection on one's own experience, etc., and the Marxist tradition—which I was more familiar with at the time—with very different starting points and premises. I advanced as far as I could, striking a balance between these two traditions.

Some things became clear to me: that the issue of the reproduction of life as a whole is central to women's struggle, and also, that there is a relationship of expropriation between men and women which I considered then to be directly proportional to the social advance of market relations. Later, I realized that the issue is much more complex, but the crucial thing was to clearly comprehend the relationship of expropriation that exists between women and men. That is, between women and men there is not just a relationship of "oppression," the term used extensively during the left-wing feminist debates of the 1980s and then diluted in the debate about "discrimination" during the '90s; rather, there is a persistent and systematic exercise of expropriation of time, energy, vitality, and other kinds of concrete—and sometimes also abstract—wealth. Understanding this was very important for me.

And it was important because I managed to understand the patriarchal nature of left-wing politics that leads to all kinds of repeated mistakes and limitations. It does so, especially when it focuses all its capacities on the objective of "occupying the government," or "taking over the state," as people used to say. If this becomes the goal, the systematic expropriation of collective energy is inscribed into the organization. These expropriated energies and capacities are then concentrated in a totally different political form where a clearly identifiable center is capable of monopolizing and concentrating to itself political decisions.

Hence, my reflections on autonomy have always been related to organizational questions. And my political practice has focused on experimenting with various organizational forms with very diverse *compañeras*.

My subsequent arguments about the cumulative importance of material, political, and symbolic autonomies is a product of that set of experiences. There is no political autonomy without material autonomy, at least partially or intermittently. And no political autonomy can sustain itself without symbolic autonomy. That is, autonomy will not exist unless one manages to repudiate—or rather "digest"—the image that the dominant order imposes on those who struggle, to expel it from the collective body and to be able to sustain the activity of signification, of assigning meaning to what has been done and what is to be done.

Perhaps, that is the most important thing I have learned in all these years. And also, the most difficult to practice systematically.

2| BEYOND THE "CAPACITY TO VETO": THE ARDUOUS JOURNEY TO PRODUCE AND REPRODUCE THE COMMON

Raquel Gutiérrez Aguilar

In memory of the community members of Totonicapán, Guatemala who were murdered on October 4, 2012 when they collectively mobilized to veto a set of legal reforms.

The capacity to veto has opened a renewed horizon of the reappropriation of social wealth. As John Holloway has written, in the beginning, there was a "NO," a cry of "*¡Basta!*," an assertion that enough is enough.[1] We witnessed a runaway outbreak of NO on this continent during the 1990s and the first years of the twenty-first century. We observed and listened closely as the rebel Zapatistas stood strong before all of Mexican society, demonstrating their extraordinary capacity to veto, their announcing a powerful NO to the ways they had been pushed aside and condemned to live amid deprivation, exclusion, and repression.

---

[1] John Holloway, *Cambiar el mundo sin tomar el poder* (Puebla/México: ICSyH-BUAP/Bajo Tierra, 2010).

We learned about the gigantic gatherings of Ecuadorian "nationalities"[2] who mobilized and said NO to the most egregious decisions of the ruling class. We were inspired by the energetic way in which the men and women of the city and the valleys of Cochabamba in Bolivia said NO to handing over water resources to a predatory transnational company, and we witnessed that same capacity again when thousands upon thousands of people from different backgrounds and nationalities refused the plundering of *their* hydrocarbons. We rejoiced in the militant, creative, and courageous way thousands and thousands of men and women in Argentina said NO to the worst forms of financial plunder imposed on them in late 2001.

I mention these cases because they are the most well-known and remarkable; however, in Latin America, for over a decade, we experienced intensifying social vetoes of varied and heterogenous types and outcomes: some were able to overthrow presidents, challenge governors, and threaten long-established landowners. Others expelled predatory transnational "service" corporations or construction companies with contracts to build airports, mines, and dams; still others safeguarded material wealth under threat from various forms of pillage.[3] Many people, a great many, rose

---

[2] In Ecuador, Indigenous groups are sometimes referred to as "nationalities." For example, the largest Indigenous political organization is called the Confederation of Indigenous Nationalities of Ecuador ([Confederación de Nacionalidades Indígenas del Ecuador] or CONAIE).—Ed.

[3] For many years, I have been working on the idea that in the recent heterogeneous struggles against neoliberal plundering, in which social antagonism is forcefully developed and deployed, what is produced collectively and, increasingly, in common, beyond anything else is the *social capacity to veto* the most unbearably aggressive assaults, dispossessions, and authoritarianisms. See Raquel Gutiérrez Aguilar, "Forma comunal y forma liberal de la

time and time again to veto the arbitrary decisions of out-
siders who ignored and stole from them. It was an acute
moment of crisis for capital with its own specificities in
these latitudes.

Following this broad, polyphonic deployment of the
social capacity to veto against the hydra of the capitalist
negation of life, a horizon opened anew for the reappropriation of commonly held wealth.[4] Half a century of the *criollo*
"welfare state" prior to the transnational liberal offensive
had undermined and concealed the deepest essence of a different form of politics: *the politics of the common*. However,
amid those tumultuous moments of the deployment of
a massive social veto and the growing reappropriation of
plundered and threatened wealth, another form of politics became both visible and audible. This form of politics,
as it derails, hinders or slows the widespread projects to
expand capitalist accumulation, simultaneously confronts
and disaggregates another approach to the political: liberal
politics.[5]

---

política," en *Pluriverso. Teoría política boliviana* (La Paz: Colección
Comuna, Editorial Muela del Diablo, 2001); Raquel Gutiérrez
Aguilar, *Democratizaciones plebeyas* (La Paz: Colección Comuna,
2002).

[4] A detailed study of Indigenous and popular uprisings and mobilizations in Bolivia between 2000 and 2005 led me to the conclusion that there was a communal-popular horizon for the political
reorganization of society, founded on the *collective and expansive
common willingness to reclaim* social wealth that had been out-
right privatized during the neoliberal years or held under a state
management system that was external to and not controlled by
society. See Raquel Gutiérrez Aguilar, *Los ritmos del Pachakuti. Levantamiento y movilización en Bolivia (2000–2005)* (México DF:
ICSyH-BUAP/Bajo Tierra Ediciones, 2009).

[5] In Mexico, "liberal" is a shifting signifier with its roots in nineteenth-century political formations. However, it refers here not to
the US equivalent of Democrat (as opposed to Republican) but

Recent years have been an extraordinary time in the Americas, as multiple and heterogeneous efforts on varied fronts have resisted the imposition of "progress" and "development," thus disrupting and fracturing the political norms founded on the mechanism of the *citizen*. This *citizen* enables a monopoly on decision-making for issues that affect everyone because all are implicated, while at the same time pretends to provide a formal equality that conceals the growing abyss between those who produce life, and are compelled to obey, and those who do not produce life, but rather profit from it and are empowered to rule.

Beginning with that "great shockwave," so visible in Chiapas, in the Ecuadorian highlands, in Cochabamba and the Aymara Altiplano, in the areas around Buenos Aires, and more discreetly in numerous corners of our continent, several countries with "progressive" governments have initiated processes of political reconstitution. These governments have made every effort to establish a *new normal* in the authority-obedience relation and in the capitalist administration of wealth to assure renewed forms of capital accumulation. The effect of this reorganization is the devaluation and fragmentation of the transformative political capacities that arose across a multiplicity of life-worlds. To this end, these national governments have formulated limited and clumsy proposals for the redistribution of certain public resources, though always a proportionally small percentage. At the same time, they have granted extensive assurances that vast amounts of material wealth will be held as private property, allowing for its exploitation by local capitalists and foreign partners.

---

rather to a politics that is connected to the state or representative democracy. Here the opposite of liberal is not "conservative" but more radical or revolutionary forms of politics.—Ed.

The fissure—or abyss or crack, to continue the dialogue with Holloway—fractured and impeded the contemporary state political order for some years, hindering extraction and exploitation.[6] This same rift allowed us to observe the meaning and the relevance of certain historical political constructions, but from a position generally hidden from view. The effect was to make not just their meanings but the things themselves malleable, while enabling spaces and times for the diffusion of shared desires, which is a vital element in both the subversion of what exists and in the collective will to produce the common.

Orienting ourselves by the practical critique of certain classic political terms made by the most energetic and far-reaching struggles of the time, we followed our hypotheses and intuitions to arrive at the following assertion: as the normalcy of capital accumulation was disrupted or fractured, alongside a collective willingness to obey outside norms, the possibility of a profound reorganization of the social body was opened up, based on the reinvention-reconfiguration of different modes of the political.

One of the contemporary political mechanisms par excellence is the Republic—*Res-publica*—understood as the place of public affairs, that is, general and far-ranging matters that concern and pertain to all those who make up a national body associated with legal forms of command and leadership. During these years of struggle, we glimpsed the possibility of reconfiguring this organizing principle into something that—to draw a contrast and a critical distinction—we might call the "Res-common."[7]

---

[6] John Holloway, *Agrietar el capitalismo: el hacer contra el trabajo* (Puebla/México: ICSyH BUAP/Bajo Tierra, 2011).

[7] Res-common here is a difficult-to-translate play on words. *Republic* comes from the Latin *res* (thing) and *publica* (of the public).

The primary features of this Res-common—created, desired, and suggested by each successive wave against the capitalist state order—are to name what should be collectively reappropriated and simultaneously to impede the order imposed by centralizing authorities that enables the monopoly of decision-making and the undebated establishment of procedures. At this point, much becomes malleable and fluid: particularly the terms for the management of the reappropriated resources and the capacity to decide on topics that concern everyone because all are implicated.[8]

So even though progressive states are re-forming currently in several countries—and some of them of a supposedly plurinational nature—they are still tragically far from and often explicitly contrary to the reappropriative horizon anchored in the logics of the common. The multitude of efforts striving in that direction are impossible to miss, even if the governing elites and their intellectual lackeys do everything in their power to disregard and negate them. Perhaps most interestingly, many efforts find form now in a variety of struggles developing in European coun-

---

A res-common would be not a public thing but a thing of the common.—Ed.

[8] I "stretch" words and their meanings because I am trying, as Luisa Muraro has written, to "think the unthinkable." In this case, I am attempting to understand what multiple collective efforts for the social reappropriation of diverse forms of material wealth and the capacity to collectively make decisions about them share. These efforts are chaotic at times, sometimes scattered, other times contradictory and fragmented, but always raucous and persevering. On this point, it is worth mentioning that Muraro seeks to untangle the idea of politics from a modern—and masculine—concept of power. See Luisa Muraro, "La independencia simbólica del poder," Ponencia al Coloquio "Poder y política no son la misma cosa" organizado por el Grupo Diótima, Universidad de Verona, 10 de octubre de 2008.

tries, though they are arising there out of conditions of even greater adversity.[9]

I believe that reading these profound, recent experiences of struggle in our lands against the grain can be useful for people who are currently fighting from their own locations and speaking their own languages. In the next section, I'll engage in a reflection on the issue of the possibilities for the production and reproduction of the common, moving beyond the capacity to veto, delving into its interior dynamics and the logics of its development.

The Horizon of the Reappropriation of Wealth: Several Considerations

The varied and polyphonic weavings—which combine a range of experiences of the production of the common—have been and continue to drive any possible reappropriation and reproduction of inherited and socially-produced wealth. This observation is particularly relevant after half a century of chimerical—and misleading—attempts at reappropriating social wealth through a range of efforts to subordinate the accumulation of capital under the control of the state.

When the efforts of large groups of women and men to defend the common and to reappropriate socially produced wealth have accepted the scission of life into two separate

---

[9] The starting conditions for the development of contemporary struggle in Europe are much harsher and more unsettled than those we face here, due to the far greater reach and increased depth of historical processes of individualization there, as well as the proliferation and predominance of commercial relations. What I mean to argue is that those fighting in Europe are forced to do so, paradoxically, under conditions of much greater vulnerability due to a severe reduction in the capacities needed for the construction of the common.

spheres, the public and the private, and then have centered their efforts on the state, they have generally achieved only limited, ephemeral, and bitter victories. As a result, new forms of concentrated, private appropriation of wealth and of the decisions and capacities to make decisions about these resources have grown like a cancer throughout the social body.

A variety of different coalitions—though somewhat isomorphic in nature—of professionalized leaders have proliferated like scabs or keloid scars in the openings, cracks, and tears generated by the struggles and revolutions against the increasingly oppressive weight of exploitation and domination. Underneath and beyond this weight, life has continued in all its fabulous variety. There, underground and partially outside of the state and capital accumulation—continually altering their combative practices, procedures, and leadership—motley and colorful associative weavings are maintained and recreated for the conservation and reproduction of life and for the defense and/or recuperation of some of the collective skills and prerogatives needed to define or establish—collectively and as much as possible independently—the directions, scales, and rhythms of life, of its care and reproduction.

In general, these weavings are the product of conversation, coordination, and the coordination of conversations between people who come together autonomously; that is, they establish their own goals, determine their scope, and set the rhythms of their own activity.[10] With this, they initially

---

[10] I use the notions of conversation, coordination, and connection in the sense that Varela and Maturana give to these expressions to explain the phenomenon of life and the cognitive abilities of human beings from a biological perspective. See Francisco J. Varela y Humberto Maturana, *El árbol del conocimiento. Las bases biológicas del entendimiento humano* (Buenos Aires: Lumen, 1984);

recover and produce—and reappropriate—a certain capacity to configure the spheres of the collective production of material life. This capacity is systematically threatened and increasingly expropriated by capital—and by the liberal political forms that follow alongside it—which undermines that capacity repeatedly by taking away the minimal conditions needed for its existence, in an attempt to convert it into work, particularly salaried work to produce capital.

These multiple, varied forms of association that produce and reproduce life trace shared traits—despite their heterogeneity —and outline certain distinguishable elements that allow us to glimpse a dynamic and a logic of the production and reproduction of life beyond capital, and therefore the state. These are the logics and dynamics of the production of the common, from which, over the last fifteen years, the most significant efforts to make visible and expand the horizon of reappropriation have sprung. These networks and their internal logics of self-production have become a phoenix for humanity: the material foundation of hope beyond dream or fantasy.

In Latin America, these weavings have been inherited, cared for, and systematically recreated and reimagined by many Indigenous peoples—particularly by Indigenous women—and also, by an endless array of heterogenous and diverse coalitions and associations focused on caring for, celebrating, and producing life. At the heart of these weavings are primarily women of different ages, accompanied at times by men, striving to subvert, break, and criticize— despite the inherent difficulty—the ties that bind them to the grotesque privileges of dominant masculinity.

Let's analyze these weavings somewhat schematically, but also with some care, as what I want to make visible, as

---

Francisco J. Varela, *Conocer: Las ciencias cognitivas. Tendencias y perspectivas* (Barcelona: Editorial GEDISA, 1988).

has been made clear in the struggles of recent years, is not only the existence but also the possibility of political relevance for an important and massive body of subjects who possess the wherewithal to restructure civilization itself: us. That is, the 99 percent of us offered nothing more than mere subsistence and suffering by capital. Despite all of this, we continue to celebrate and care for life, as we reproduce it daily.

Everything is not capital, even in a world where practically everything that exists has been or is in the process of being privatized—that is, appropriated by the private sector—for the production of capital (from water to knowledge, from technology to leisure time, from plants to seeds and minerals, and even humans themselves as they are continually made less sacred and more into objects or things). Holloway argues that *making* is what is actually not capital (2001). And *making* is repeatedly captured and submitted, though never completely, to the logic of capital. That is what creates work's never-ending cycle: the prison of salaried labor or imposed labor. *Making* is the substance that capital subjects, captures, and absorbs repeatedly in apparently endless loops; despite this, sometimes brutal, disciplining impasses exist within this dynamic, like the emergence of mass unemployment happening now in Europe and the United States. A crucial question concerns the *conditions of possibility for making and its connection* to the very conditions through which *making* might be able to stabilize sufficient spheres for its continued existence and for its possible expansion. That is, to produce, care for and reproduce more energetic and fast-flowing torrents in the *social flows of making*. These minimal conditions are barely sufficient in some moments though, at others, they become astonishingly elastic in their capacity for development and find their form in the multifaceted and polyphonic logics of the production of the common. The common—its recognition, care, and systematic production—are the conditions of possibility of *making* and of the expanding link to a *making* that builds into a powerful current that erodes and traps the accumulation of capital while it dissolves the vertical and privatized relations of the hierarchical world that constitute it. The *common* as a multifaceted, diffuse, and pliable crystallization of *making*—under constant threat of further exploitation and alienation—constitutes not just the minimal material conditions for the initial development of *making*, but also, beyond a certain threshold in its tense and varied connection to other *makings*, opens the horizon of a common reappropriation of material wealth to convert it into the source of its own power.

The common, then, is not just the departure point for the critical development of *making*, but also at the same time in its double extension—of the common and of *making*—traces its horizon. It does so not as a model, but rather as a path, as an imagined and produced passage, as an itinerary for its own self-reproduction.

Logics of the Production of the Common *Beyond-Against and Beyond Capital* and Systematic Tensions Between Two Contradictory Political Forms: The Liberal and the Communitarian[11]

---

[11] The idea of the production of the common as something that is beyond-against and beyond capital and, thus, connected to Holloway's formulation of a horizon of an unfolding antagonism, which is always connected to everyday life, was the collective product of the autonomous seminar "Emancipation Pathways" and it was developed in particular by Lucía Linsalata; see her book *El ethos comunal en la política boliviana. Una aproximación a las formas comunales de la política en el mundo aymara boliviano* (Mexico City: EAE Editorial, 2012).

Considering the argument so far, we can affirm now that the production of the common is founded in a "female we," a "*nosotras*."[12] This is a female we whose meaning goes far beyond the negotiated agglomeration of "I's" in which we are encapsulated by modern civil codes in almost all the nations of the world, recognizing ourselves instead as a "collective figure." This female we is a starting point that is simultaneously inherited and produced, that is, that precedes us and which at the same time provides us with tools for its reinvention.[13] A female we that increases our capacity to desire *beyond and against* the multiple offerings of what exists as merchandise and as identity. A female we that holds us, provides us with shelter, and has our backs. A female we that nourishes us. A female we that inherits, produces, and reproduces the common can be of many different classes; it can take on different forms. And yet, in the most energetic moments of struggle, when social antagonism develops and illuminates everything around it, it allows us to perceive what is historically hidden and denied on a daily basis; at that moment, it becomes possible to explore some of its expressions, its ways of being and of unfolding, its complex

---

[12] From here on, I will use "*nosotras*"—the feminine form of we— to refer to the varied associative weavings of women and men that produce the common and who, even when they are stripped of everything they have produced, continue producing it with their labor or repeatedly reinvent ways of doing so. Employing this inversion in the charged use of the gendered first-person plural in Spanish has as its goal to make visible the fact that the politics and logics of the common are embodied by people—men and women—who necessarily criticize the order and the modern dominant masculine sensibility that is historically linked to the accumulation of capital and the constitution of the state. On this topic, see Silvia Federici, *Calibán y la bruja. Mujeres, cuerpo y acumulación originaria* (Buenos Aires: Tinta Limón, 2011).

[13] On this topic, see Muraro, "La independencia simbólica del poder."

and almost infinitely varied ways of producing and repro-
ducing the world.

The overflowing energy of *making* in moments of
struggle makes us feel and see everything that once might
have been forgotten. What a person, a woman[14] perceives
intensely in those moments of common strength, although
it is difficult to render it intelligible as a communicable
experience, is the most intimate dynamic of multiple conversations and reciprocal connections that enable precisely
that strength, that commonly produced—or reinvented—
capacity to furnish common goals and to mutually connect
with one another to work towards achieving them. The
dynamic of the common in everyday terms, to present my
view in a schematic way, is woven together through the following logic:

1) The re-discovery and re-production of a sense of
   collective inclusion, many times inherited, although
   always re-generated through systematic deliberation
   on an intention or a collective goal. The question
   becomes: Who produces, re-produces, re-discovers

---

[14] Gutiérrez uses "*una*" here, "*una percibe*," which is a difficult
thing to express in English. It is perhaps referring to one person,
one feminine person or femme person, or one woman who finds
herself in a particular moment of intense perception in the midst
of struggle. As Gutiérrez reminds us, the "*nosotras*" is not made
up of "I's." And if it is not composed of individual first persons,
it is perhaps made up of a conglomeration of "unas," female ones.
Though later, Gutiérrez complicated this idea further by stating
that men and women can belong within a "nosotras" thus opening
the way to thinking about "una" here as indicating an inversion of
who/what comes first and not mapping onto a specific gender, allowing for a multiplicity of genders to inhabit that word. —Trans.

or amplifies the common? And to what end? This sense of collective inclusion is cemented through the creation of mechanisms of equalization and/or equilibrium—that are not merely formal—in relation to what is being produced and/or what is desired to be produced in common. Forms of collectively producing the relation of "being part of" are deliberated upon and then rehearsed, not through codes or terms of exclusion but rather of *some sense of inclusion.*

2) Beginning with this initial sense of inclusion, codes of relating are carefully instituted (general obligations, concrete dynamics of reciprocal obligations,[15] terms of collective usufruct of what was produced in this way). Norms are recovered and promulgated that lead and guide both the relationship of each part to the common, as well as the bilateral or multilateral relationship between "parts."

3) Gradually, specific modes arise and stabilize for regulating internal conflicts and for developing and modifying the goals of the common.[16]

---

[15] We should note that, in general, the dynamics of production-reproduction of the common are founded on sets of obligations, which, when enacted, guarantee usufruct rights, but not property rights. Despite this, in almost all the cases studied so far, these obligations are accepted autonomously: that is, each *part*—each domestic unit in the case of the weavings of some Indigenous peoples—decides to take on an obligation in order to strengthen, at least initially, their own capacity to obtain something together and in collaboration with others.

[16] The schematic presentation of this logic might seem very abstract. It is based on research into multiple, everyday practices of the reproduction of life, of the organization of celebrations and parties, of the repeated production of forms of association to confront and overcome needs both in Mexico, as well as in Bolivia, Guatemala, Ecuador, Chile, and Peru. The work of Lucía Linsalata

Primarily, this dynamic unfolds, as would be expected, through the circulation of the word, in conversation to agree on goals and then to determine ways to reach them. This is why the production of the common is intimately linked both to collective meetings in assembly, as well as to general, informal deliberation about the goals to be proposed and the methods to reach them. The oldest and most reliable mode of assuring the circulation of the collective power-of-making is to freely exchange words in the assembly, which is recognized as the place for reaching agreements and required collective decisions and as a space where the goals of the female we who is speaking can be clarified. This collective power-of-making is increasingly held in common, as it is recovered, reconstructed, and reinvented to avoid its concentration-monopolization, which, interpreted through this lens, is nothing more than the seizure or private appropriation of the capacity for making and reaching goals, as determined by a group.

This is the source of the rich and varied forms of administration and self-regulation of the common, that is, of the *politics of the common*, which are conserved by Indigenous peoples as an inheritance and abundance that has still not been entirely erased, though it has been brutally assaulted. The politics of the common, at least in general terms, is clearly in opposition to the dispossession or the private appropriation of what everyone produces, including the privatization of the capacity for decision-making that is welded into modern liberal forms of politics and the political.

On this last issue, allow me to quickly address a set of ideas that highlight this contrast:

---

includes an interesting explication of these issues. See Linsalata, *El ethos comunal en la política boliviana.*

Liberal form of politics and the political	Communal / communitarian form of politics and the political
Establishes the individual as the starting point. Afterwards, it institutes—with permission—procedures for the varied aggregation of individuals.	Establishes a "*nosotras*" [female we], to develop its activity; that is, this form is founded in collective life. Also establishes varied guarantees to assure distinct arenas for individual autonomy.
Sets up mediations to assure command relationships. The nexus of liberal representation—mediation par excellence—is the *delegation of the capacity to decide* on issues of collective interest and importance, which are concentrated in a principal leader. Institutes procedural formats and specific timeframes that ensure the longevity of this monopolized concentration of collective decision-making capacity.	Designates prominent figures—e.g., spokespeople, leaders—to organize common activities and goals, while simultaneously attempting to limit command relationships by *not delegating* or not handing over collective and individual decision-making capacity. For this reason, it ties the concept of service to the figure of the organizer-authority.

Internal logic and rhythms of this political form reinforce internal hierarchies within the aggregation of individuals. These hierarchies tend to be exclusionary and rigid.

As long as it is linked to securing and expanding capital accumulation, repeatedly ignores the needs and activities aimed at the reproduction of life. It silos off the means of production where those who are not in power find ways to secure their existence.

The liberal form of politics and the political determines and limits—it prescribes and fixes—the possibilities for individual and collective existence and transformation. Simultaneously, it ignores the care and maintenance work that allow for the existence of all people in a particular moment. In summary, liberal politics tends to destroy and prescribe, in addition to establishing hierarchies and excluding.

Internal logic and rhythms of this political form tend toward equilibrium. What they make visible and practice is the *destituent* capacity that resides in the "nosotras," in the fundamental figure of the collective. For this reason, they create malleable or fluid—never noncontradictory—possibilities for collective self-regulation.

Focuses its attention on the reproduction of life and on the creation of the means necessary to secure it. In that sense, conserves and cares for what it has, while simultaneously trying out new forms of collective appropriation.

Communal forms of politics and the political are intensely focused on the conservation of what exists, in the sense of caring for the material wealth that it still has at its disposal. Nonetheless, they are not immutable nor impervious to transformations: they simultaneously conserve what exists and—gradually and arduously—create possibilities for the expansion of its enjoyment.

The Politics of the Common Opens Horizons of Collective Reappropriation of Social Wealth

This essay set out to explore the question of possibilities and political horizons beyond the use and tumultuous development of the social capacity to veto, to stall or inhibit the most brutal attacks of capital and its accumulation upon life and reproduction. Through an investigation into recent Latin American history, we have argued that an increasingly common, luminous collective horizon has appeared allowing for the reappropriation of social wealth, as occurred previously during the most intense years of the Russian Revolution, during the Chinese Revolution and various others. A horizon is opened for the reappropriation of material wealth created and preserved collectively and for the retaking of decision-making power related to issues that affect everyone in common, beyond the last few centuries' consecrated state forms.

The conditions of possibility for this tumultuous overflowing of making *beyond* and *against and beyond* capital and the state rest on the capacity to produce, nurture, and reproduce the common. A new common sense of assemblies and town councils as spaces for deliberation and reaching agreements, where goals are clarified and steps, rhythms, and scales are established, and the material capacity to put decisions into action is centered.[17]

The vertiginous creative hurricane that disorganizes, inhibits, and destroys what currently exists as prison, as lack and limit, points us towards another path. It calls

---

[17] I appreciate the discussions we have had in the "Alternative Modernities" seminar, where time and time again we have reflected together on the significant issue of scale—spatial dimensions—and rhythms—heterogenous patterns in time—in relation to common human creations.

us together to traverse it while, simultaneously, it suffers systematic harassment and capture. The reappropriative horizon in Latin America is presently, and once again, fragmented into multiple, scattered struggles, regathering their strength in varied efforts to put into practice the production of the common on an everyday basis. These efforts open us to the field of resonances in this ancient, recovered desire.

To a certain degree, we are currently trapped in that new normalcy imposed by an array of progressive governments. This normalcy is founded, primarily, on the devaluation, exploitation, and even repression of desires to construct and expand the common and of efforts guided by the horizon of the common reappropriation of social wealth. The flame of this desire, nonetheless, has been lit now in many other places. This is the reason why reflecting on what we have managed to envision and also on what we have still not been able to achieve can serve as, I hope, a contribution to all those who are standing up and in movement.[18]

---

[18] This essay was originally written in Autumn 2012 in Puebla, Mexico.

3| PRODUCING THE COMMON: COMMUNITARIAN WEAVINGS AND FORMS OF THE POLITICAL

Raquel Gutiérrez Aguilar

This essay was written in Puebla, September 2017.

This essay proposes to do two things: to provide an organized overview of the multiple strands of reflection we are weaving together among those of us who are—or have been—part of the Permanent Research Seminar "Communitarian Weavings and Forms of the Political" in the Postgraduate Program in Sociology at the Institute of Social Sciences and Humanities within the Autonomous University of Puebla.[1] Second, to organize and present the partial conclusions that we have arrived at collectively. The objective here is to provide an account of our own work process in terms of research and education and present our findings and shared ideas, which have typically been presented in a more dispersed and fragmentary way due

---

[1] The permanent seminar "Communitarian Weavings and Forms of the Political" is coordinated by Mina L. Navarro, Lucía Linsalata, and Raquel Gutiérrez Aguilar, who are professors and researchers at the ICSyH-BUAP.

to the conditions of individual authorship imposed by the academy.

The desire to understand and, to the extent possible, to practice the heterogenous and manifold community-based forms of the regeneration of bonds and thinking that are cultivated on this continent has been ongoing for some time. In particular, this desire arises out of the effort made over several decades to understand, document, support, and participate in diverse Indigenous and popular community-based struggles, primarily in Bolivia and also in Mexico, Guatemala, Ecuador, Peru, Chile, and Colombia. Through these experiences, we learned to distinguish the communitarian traits of specific forms of struggle, always unique and distinct, but at the same time parallel and interconnected. We contrasted these traits identified across very diverse contexts with liberal forms of politics,[2] especially with what we consider to be the backbone of that political form: the organization of public life around the *delegation* of the collective capacity to intervene in general affairs that concern everyone because they affect everyone.[3]

In opposition to this, a shared trait we find in communitarian political forms is that these *struggles for the*

---

[2] As we noted in the prior chapter, in Mexico "liberal" is a sifting signifier with its roots in nineteenth-century political formations. However, it refers here not to the US equivalent of Democrat (as opposed to Republican) but rather to a politics that in connected to the state or representative democracy. Here the opposite of liberal is not "conservative" but more radical or revolutionary forms of politics.—Ed.

[3] Raquel Gutiérrez Aguilar, "Forma comunal y forma liberal de la política," en *Pluriverso. Teoría política boliviana* (La Paz: Colección Comuna, Editorial Muela del Diablo, 2001); Raquel Gutiérrez Aguilar, *Los ritmos del Pachakuti. Movilización y levantamiento indígena-popular en Bolivia (2000–2005)* (Buenos Aires: Tinta Limón/Universidad Internacional de Andalucía, 2008).

common[4] are almost always organized and made manifest through collective efforts to defend the material and symbolic conditions necessary to guarantee the reproduction of common life. This similarity will become a starting point for our reflections. In this process, we must acknowledge the importance of the work of Silvia Federici in the formulation of our own arguments.[5] We have enjoyed a fruitful conversation with Federici ever since we were lucky enough to meet her and to begin a dialogue with her ideas. Organizing our thinking around the axis of collective efforts to ensure the material and symbolic reproduction of human and non-human life has led us to our own "Copernican revolution." As we were used to placing the accumulation of capital and its state-centric politics at the center of our analysis—as the dominant discourse dictates—it has meant a lot to us, as women,[6] to reconnect with the radical feminist thinking of the 1970s, which, in multiple ways, illuminated social and political realms which, for classical Marxism, were hidden within the opaque world of consumption.

As is customary within capitalist, patriarchal and colonial modernity, thought is typically centered on the

---

[4] Mina Lorena Navarro Trujillo, *Luchas por lo común. Antagonismo social contra el despojo capitalista de los bienes naturales en México* (Puebla/México: Bajo Tierra/Instituto de Ciencias Sociales y Humanidades-BUAP, 2015).

[5] Silvia Federici, *Calibán y la bruja. Mujeres, cuerpo y acumulación originaria* (México: Pez en el Árbol/Tinta Limón, 2013); Silvia Federici, *La revolución feminista inacabada. Mujeres, reproducción social y lucha por lo común* (México: Escuela Calpulli, 2013).

[6] Whenever this particular text in the English translation says "we," it is important to read this as a feminine "*nosotras*," that is, as a collectivity of women (and some men) engaged in intellectual and activist work. As it is often awkward to create this "female we" in English, let this note stand in for that feminist first-person plural pronoun.—Trans.

production and accumulation of capital, and the language used is generated for thinking in that context; in this way, processes of production and consumption are elucidated, and their interrelationships are investigated. By locating capitalist accumulation as the starting point, the vast galaxy of material, emotional, and symbolic activities and processes that occur and unfold in areas of human activity that are not immediately related to capitalist production is made invisible and dismissed, even as they continue despite constraints and attacks. Both the creative and productive processes that sustain daily human and nonhuman life and the set of activities and tasks aimed at procreation and supporting future generations are hidden and are considered "anomalies." Human capacities for generating various types of social bonds, which extend far beyond the market relations associated with the production of value, are also unacknowledged and dismissed, even though such practices almost always develop within the constraints imposed by the expansively aggressive logic of the valorization of value. All these social landscapes abound with collective practices that sustain daily life, which are dismissed and made invisible by the productivist gaze of contemporary capitalism. These are precisely the landscapes and practices that have become the starting point for our work.

Our focus has been on those dynamic Indigenous struggles for territory, for the common appropriation of expropriated material wealth, and for self-governance, as well as on a significant portion of the wide array of struggles historically led by women. We have learned to make certain distinctions and to assert that within these movements everyday relationships are regenerated and re-actualized which are not entirely mediated by capital or patriarchy. In addition, these movements develop forms of production that establish guidelines for renewed forms of obligation towards the collective and guarantees for the enjoyment of shared and cultivated material wealth, subverting the colonial legacy time and again. Thus, we name political forms that, across many levels, are different from and in opposition to the specific and rigid *usos y costumbres* [practices and customs] of liberal capitalist modernity.

In our working group, we maintain that these two characteristics—the guarantee of the material and symbolic reproduction of collective life and the multitudinous communitarian political practices that regulate it—are at the center of an array of communitarian-popular struggles that both construct and illuminate paths of social emancipation beyond the logics of the modern state and capital accumulation.[7]

As all these creative and productive processes focused on ensuring the material and symbolic reproduction of life have been ongoing for centuries, they are always circumscribed and threatened by the relentless pressures of the accumulative logic of capital in all its forms (mercantile, industrial, agro-industrial, extractive, manufacturing, financial, criminal). Our thinking is always oriented towards understanding the multitudinous and heterogeneous struggles against the explicit separations, constraints, and aggressions that repeatedly entangle, hinder, or disrupt the practical capacities and knowledge that people possess—and are capable of cultivating—as part of diverse cultural weavings.

Based on these ideas, we have crafted a methodological framework that is open to the always-changing collective construction that unfolds in these struggles, which refuses, in

---

[7] Raquel Gutiérrez Aguilar, *Horizonte comunitario-popular. Antagonismo y producción de lo común en América Latina* (México: Benemérita Universidad Autónoma de Puebla, 2015); Lucía Linsalata, *El ethos comunal en la política boliviana. Una aproximación a las formas comunales de la política en el mundo aymara boliviano* (México DF: EAE Editorial, 2012); Navarro, *Luchas por lo común.*

any way, a closed conceptual structure. Rather, starting with an account of the differences and specificities of various and heterogenous social practices of everyday struggle and centered around the two aforementioned axes—the guarantee of the material and symbolic reproduction of collective life and the variety of political forms for the regulation of these tasks—our work investigates similarities in these practices, their ambiguities and contradictions. In addition, we look at capacities for resistance and struggle embedded within them and the difficulties they repeatedly face as they are systematically contained, attacked, threatened, and subsumed into distinct processes of neo(liberal)-colonial capitalist reconfiguration, which aims to expand the social space and the life force available for capital accumulation, resorting to increasingly more widespread and brutal forms of violence.[8]

This perspective has led us to lay out our thought processes along two analytical axes. On the one hand, we distinguish between the *quality of time*, both of the everyday and the social, during ordinary and extraordinary moments. In addition, we look at the *quality of time* as it is related to practices linked to the sustaining of collective life and the multiple forms of (self-)regulation of these shared practices of social activity. That is, we analyze the constellation of political forms that organize and drive these collective activities.

As we carry out our research and educational work, we use at least four approaches that are interlinked, though each one is specific. The first approach draws on what has been learned from an array of struggles led by various Indigenous movements in Latin America,[9] tracing what

---

[8] Dawn Paley, *Drug War Capitalism* (Oakland: AK Press, 2014).

[9] Raquel Gutiérrez Aguilar y Fabiola Escárzaga (coords.), *Movimiento indígena en América Latina: resistencia y proyecto alternativo*, vol. I (México: Casa Juan Pablos/BUAP/UACM/UNAM/

has happened during extraordinary moments of organized struggle and documenting the expansive way that everyday community practices—seen as apolitical from the dominant point of view—have entered public space, subverting and/or impeding contemporary structures of domination and exploitation.[10]

The second and third approaches in our research have focused on the meticulous study of everyday forms of production and the sustaining of the communal, understood as the practice and regeneration of self-regulated bonds of interdependence. The nurturing of these bonds is an everyday, repeated activity and our work has illuminated the different political traits of such collective actions.[11] Our most significant contribution in this area has been our thinking on *communitarian politicity*, which is learned and cultivated daily through meaningful and complicated activities carried out individually and collectively, repeatedly and continually, within the multiple weavings of the reproduction of life. This is despite the extreme dismissal and equally persistent invisibilization of their political nature, by an array of modern regimes of governance and domination. This approach has also clearly drawn on the contributions of two contemporary Latin American philosophers: Bolívar

---

GDF, 2005); Raquel Gutiérrez Aguilar y F. Escárzaga, J. Carrillo, E. Capece y Borries Nehe (coords.), *Movimiento indígena en América Latina: resistencia y proyecto alternativo*, vol. II (México: Casa Juan Pablos/CEAM/UAM/BUAP/UACM/GDF/Diakonía/CIDES/UMSA/UPEA, 2006).

[10] Gutiérrez, *Los ritmos*; Gutiérrez, *Horizonte comunitario-popular.*

[11] Lucía Linsalata, *Cuando manda la asamblea. Lo comunitario-popular en Bolivia: una mirada desde los sistemas comunitarios de agua de Cochabamba* (La Paz: SOCEE/Autodeterminación/Fundación, April 2015); Gladys Tzul Tzul, *Sistemas de gobierno comunitario indígena. Mujeres y tramas de parentesco en Chuimeq'ena'* (Guatemala: SOCEE/Tz'ikin, 2016).

Echeverría and Luis Tapia. From different angles, each has shed light on ancient political knowledge systems that are embedded in the multifaceted networks of interdependence, almost always local, that on occasion develop into powerful emancipatory struggles. Our perspective owes much to Tapia's thinking about "savage politics"[12] and the critical recovery of the notion of "use-value" by Echeverría.[13]

The fourth approach has focused on researching the struggles to guarantee the reproduction of collective life in the face of threats and dispossession, understanding these as recurrent struggles for the common that nurture daily the political capacities deployed in extraordinary moments—such as when a community faces an imminent threat of dispossession of what had been until then commonly-held assets.[14] This approach has been informed by a constant dialogue with critical or open Marxism, which has also found a home in the postgraduate program in Sociology at the ICSyH-BUAP, primarily due to the work of John Holloway[15] and Sergio Tischler.[16]

---

[12] Luis Tapia, *Política salvaje* (La Paz: Comuna/Muela del Diablo/ Clacso, 2008).

[13] Bolívar Echeverría, *Valor de uso y utopía* (México: Siglo XXI, 1998).

[14] Mina Lorena Navarro Trujillo y Claudia Composto (comps.), *Territorios en disputa. Despojo capitalista, luchas en defensa de los bienes comunes naturales y alternativas emancipatorias para América Latina* (México: Bajo Tierra Ediciones, 2014); Raquel Gutiérrez Aguilar y F. Escárzaga, J. Carrillo, E. Capece y Borries Nehe (coords.), *Movimiento indígena en América Latina: resistencia y proyecto alternativo*, vol. III (México: UAM-BUAP-CIESAS-CEAM, 2014).

[15] John Holloway, *Cambiar el mundo sin tomar el poder* (Puebla/ México: ICSyH-BUAP/Bajo Tierra, 2010); John Holloway, *Agrietar el capitalismo. El hacer contra el trabajo* (Puebla/México: ICSyH-BUAP/Bajo Tierra, 2011).

[16] Sergio Tischler, *Memoria, tiempo y sujeto* (Guatemala: BUAP/ F&G, 2005).

All this work has allowed us to weave together arguments that identify *the collective human capacity to produce the common*[17] and to carefully consider that capacity, understanding it as *a struggle against the extensive imposition of separations and ruptures* upon both ancient and reimagined forms of the reproduction of life. These separations and ruptures are always instruments for capital accumulation[18] and for the reinscription of political and social hierarchies that reinforce patriarchal and colonial traits in our societies. In dialogue with the arguments of critical Marxism, which informs our thinking with concepts like the "social flow of making" or the "social flow of struggle" or rebellion, we return to Marxist distinctions that were well-analyzed by Echeverría—like abstract labor and concrete labor. We also attempt to make visible and to amplify the "flows of concrete labor"[19] and ask after the conditions of sustainability

---

[17] Raquel Gutiérrez Aguilar, Mina Lorena Navarro, y Lucía Linsalata, "Producing the Common: Clues to Understand 'the Political,'" in *Social Sciences for an Other Politics: Women Theorising without Parachutes*, ed. Ana Cecilia Dinerstein (Cham, Switzerland: Palgrave Macmillan, 2016).

[18] Mina Lorena Navarro Trujillo, "Una perspectiva socioecológica para pensar el despojo múltiple y las separaciones del capital sobre la vida," en *Naturaleza, territorio y conflicto en la trama capitalista contemporánea*, 93–109, comp. Diego Pérez, Gonzalo Barrios, y Ezequiel Acsebrud (Buenos Aires: Extramuros Ediciones/Theomai Libros, 2018).

[19] Raquel Gutiérrez Aguilar y Huáscar Salazar Lohman, "Reproducción comunitaria de la vida. Pensando la transformación social en el presente," *el Apantle, Revista de Estudios Comunitarios, 'Común ¿para qué?'* #1 (Puebla/México: SOCEE, octubre 2015).

of "making the common" in ordinary times and in rural areas but also in urban contexts.[20]

This has been the starting point for us to engage in countless dialogues with other compañeros and militants in Mexico, Bolivia, Ecuador, and Guatemala, as well as in countries that do not share an explicitly Indigenous-communitarian framework, like Argentina, Uruguay, Italy, Spain, England, and in the United States in California and New York. A relevant aspect of these extensive networks of conversations, which we have contributed to along with many others, is that our most free-flowing dialogues have been with women: academics, researchers, activists, and militant organizers. This has once again led us to engage with the work of Silvia Federici in its more adamantly feminist incarnations, or what is often referred to in the Rio de la Plata region as a "feminism of the common."

What I have provided so far then is, in broad terms, a concise description of what we do and have done so far; this work has brought us together as a working group nested within a public Mexican university. Now, as concisely as possible, we'll present some of the lessons we have learned.

First, community and popular-communitarian struggles, many with Indigenous roots, vigorously unfolded across the continent for many decades throughout the twentieth century.[21] These struggles have challenged and

---

[20] Mina Lorena Navarro Trujillo, *Hacer común contra la fragmentación: experiencias de autonomía urbana* (Puebla/México: Instituto de Ciencias Sociales y Humanidades-BUAP, 2016).

[21] Lucía Linsalata (coord.), *Lo comunitario-popular en México: desafíos, tensiones y posibilidades* (Puebla/México: Instituto de Ciencias Sociales y Humanidades-BUAP, 2016); Gutiérrez, *Horizonte comunitario-popular*; Raquel Gutiérrez Aguilar, Huáscar Salazar Lohman, y Gladys Tzul Tzul, "Leer el siglo XX a contrapelo. Constelaciones de historias comunitarias de luchas por territorios y autogobierno en Bolivia y Guatemala," en *el Apantle, Revista*

provoked a crisis within: 1) the nation-state with its amalgamation of colonial-republican-liberal domination and capitalist exploitation, 2) the structure of agrarian ownership and consolidated wealth that sustains longstanding relationships of dominance and political patronage, 3) the wave of new and *multiple dispossessions* of material wealth and political capabilities that came hand in hand with the neoliberal backlash of recent decades.[22]

Generally, in the most protracted and radical struggles led by Indigenous people, these three pillars of domination and exploitation have not been simultaneously brought into crisis. Rather, the structures of domination have been rebuilt again and again out of what has remained intact, almost always through expropriation—and semantic and political capture—of the most deep-seated aspirations in play during moments of active struggle. On this topic, Salazar has also extensively studied how the process of community social struggle is being "expropriated" to reinstate a patriarchal-capitalist order disguised as plurinationality, particularly in the case of Bolivia.[23]

In recent years, we have focused on documenting how the transformative energies regenerated in emancipatory community struggles have been brutally attacked through: 1) contemporary forms of war and terror ravaging territories and decimating the communitarian weavings that inhabit

---

de Estudios Comunitarios, '¿Común cómo? Lógicas y situaciones' #2 (Puebla/México: SOCEE, octubre 2016).

[22] Navarro, *Luchas por lo común.*

[23] Raquel Gutiérrez Aguilar y Huáscar Salazar Lohman, "Reproducción comunitaria de la vida. Pensando la transformación social en el presente," en *el Apantle, Revista de Estudios Comunitarios, 'Común ¿para qué?'* #1 (Puebla/México: SOCEE, octubre 2015).

them by murdering and disappearing children[24]; 2) liberal policies articulated around issues of identity that have built a rigid, sophisticated legal and procedural framework, both to divert and appropriate collective power by channeling it toward negotiations about the recognition of these identities, and to reinstate reinvigorated forms of dispossession and political patronage, constantly paired with endless bargaining over unfulfilled rights.[25] These have been the two main paths of a virulent and widespread *strategy of expanded counterinsurgency*,[26] whose central aim, in our view, has been to obstruct and attempt to close off the creative lifelines of ongoing community struggle, blurring and partially confusing the horizons of communitarian-popular transformation.[27]

Another interwoven line of investigation has delved into how these struggles are remembered, tracing the tension between memory and forgetting, primarily in dialogue with E.P. Thompson. In this context, what is central for us is the concept of the *organization of experience* that unfolds within traditions of struggle and is almost always rooted in specific territories.[28] Through language and the activa-

---

[24] Dawn Paley, "La guerra en México a contrapelo: contrainsurgencia ampliada versus lo popular," *el Apantle: Revista de Estudios Comunitarios* (Puebla/México: SOCCEE/Pez en el árbol (octubre 2016): 181–197; Itandehui Reyes Díaz, "Los cercamientos de los cuerpos-territorios y la lucha contra el feminicidio en Ecatepec," Master's thesis, Puebla, BUAP, 2017.

[25] Vilma Rocío Almendra Quiguanas, "Emancipación Nasa: luchas, contradicciones y desafíos. Cooptación, asimilación y captura para revertir el horizonte emancipatorio," Master's thesis in Sociology, Puebla, ICSyH-BUAP, 2016.

[26] Paley, "La guerra en México a contrapelo."

[27] Gutiérrez, *Horizonte comunitario-popular.*

[28] Elia Méndez García, *De relámpagos y recuerdos . . . Minería y tradición de lucha serrana por lo común* (Guadalajara: Universidad de Guadalajara/CIESAS/Cátedra Jorge Alonso, 2017).

tion of memory by the power of shared recollection held in conversation, what is recovered is not just the experience of past struggles, but also shared meanings, which, precisely by "making meaning," allow individual experience to intertwine with those of others, contributing to the organization of common experience. In fact, by sharing words illuminated by memory, this is how experience can "self-organize" into a common experience. Hence the decisive role of language in the creation and the regeneration of bonds.

Along this journey, we have moved from a reflection on the practical implications, contradictions and ambiguities that occur during extraordinary moments of active struggle to an understanding of the specific and critical politicity cultivated in the communal weavings that sustain material and symbolic life each day and during extraordinary moments. With this in mind, we have woven together three analytical registers to deepen our understanding of the communal.

The first analytic: the communal is not necessarily Indigenous; to be Indigenous is not necessarily communal

We have followed two lines of thought as we furthered a discussion about the not necessarily Indigenous nature of the communal. First, we reflected on our participation in the Water War in Cochabamba, Bolivia from 2000 to 2001, which was characterized by a powerful social convergence of at least three distinct experiences of resistance and struggle: irrigators in the inter-Andean valleys of Cochabamba with communitarian backgrounds, the Federation of Factory Workers of Cochabamba with its popular-labor union framework, and the men and women who built independent systems for drinking water, mainly scattered in the peripheral areas of the city with their communitarian-popular structure. The political density, and creativity, of this multitude of political experiences and practices opened unprecedented possibilities for the production of shared horizons of meaning, but also for the convergence of different groups willing to generate fully anticapitalist social relations and, from there, tensely antistate ones. Those struggles highlighted the expansive quality of the communitarian outside of the Indigenous realm, demonstrating the strategic condition of its forms of connection and production of agreement.

Secondly, we pursued an investigation into the long-dismissed communitarian Indigenous struggles in Guatemala, which for more than a decade were blocked by the loss of some of their most vital transformational aspects. This blockage occurred following the recognition of certain cultural rights by the Guatemalan state, as it was reconstituted following the 1996 Peace Accords. As critically examined by Tzul, these accords ignored matters having to do with land and water ownership and their use by the various Indigenous peoples of the country, as well as completely disregarding their own diverse systems of governance, such as the collective production of agreements, of political decision-making, and of authority.[29]

The critical analysis of these two experiences over time was joined with a reflection on the scope and limitations of Indigenous movements—primarily in Bolivia, Mexico, Ecuador, and recently in Guatemala—as they either transformed or became entangled in state structures of political domination. All this thinking prompted us to clearly distinguish between the register of ethnicity as it is determined from the outside and as it identifies—and therefore enables the state administration of—Indigenous peoples in Latin America—and the communitarian register of subversion and challenging the political and economic order of

---

[29] Tzul, *Sistemas de gobierno comunitario indígena*.

domination that alter the social textures and meanings of multiple collective actions that on occasion lead to new and unusual alliances.

This analytical distinction in no way denies the fact that Indigenous peoples of the Americas have been the ones who have most persistently cultivated the collective capacity to produce and to care for the common. We do not deny this, but rather recognize it fully and strive to learn from the contributions of the historical and contemporary struggles of Indigenous peoples. Nevertheless, we do emphasize the fact that the ethnic register of analysis is not necessarily communitarian, and the communitarian and the capacity to produce the common are not necessarily grounded in ethnically distinct communities. This distinction has led us to investigate the communitarian and collective capacities to produce the common more deeply.

The second analytic: the communitarian is a social relation to be practiced and cultivated

The communitarian or communitarian-popular analytic of social transformation has allowed us to see the possibilities and challenges that appear in the course of social struggles led, primarily, though not exclusively, by Indigenous peoples, which, in other analyses, are overlooked or not clearly understood. This is the argument, for example, in Gladys Tzul's critical discussion of the practices and political objectives of what is called the Maya Movement in Guatemala.[30] She highlights two key characteristics of the political power of the communitarian weavings of Totonicapán: the centrality of collective work or *k'ax k'ol*, which continually reproduces communitarian weavings, and the ability of those same weavings to each year regenerate their consti-

---

[30] Tzul, *Sistemas de gobierno comunitario indígena.*

tutive bonds, reinvigorating forms of authority inside local systems of governance that regulate the care and use of available material wealth. In a parallel fashion, Linsalata's work on independent communitarian drinking water systems in Cochabamba also places collective and creative communitarian service work at the center of her reflection, as the primary source of the capacity to produce the common, linking it to the guarantee of the reproduction of life—in this case, access to water—and the cultivation of autonomous political forms.[31]

From here we turned our attention to the self-produced quality—the autopoiesis—of communitarian weavings and the cultivation of their specific political capacities. In addition, we began to focus on the centrality of distinctive sorts of collective work linked to the material and symbolic reproduction of life for the production of the common—in other words, to care for, benefit from, or regenerate what is shared—and to generate and cultivate forms of regulation and governance of the common based on the co-production of agreements that both are binding and create non-liberal forms of authority. On this point, we learned a great deal from Jaime Martínez Luna on communal work: "Communality—as we call the behavior that emerges out of the dynamics of the reproduction of our ancestral and contemporary organizational system—is grounded in work, never in discourse.[32] That is, there is decision-making work (the assembly), coordination work (the post or

---

[31] Lucía Linsalata, *Cuando manda la asamblea. Lo comunitario-popular en Bolivia: una mirada desde los sistemas comunitarios de agua de Cochabamba* (La Paz: SOCEE/Autodeterminación/Fundación, April 2015).

[32] Jaime Martínez Luna, *Textos sobre el camino andado* (Oaxaca, México, CSEIIO-CAMPO, 2013), 79–89.

cargo), construction work (the *tequio*), and pleasure work (the celebration)."[33]

Our critical work has centered involvement in, documentation of, and reflection on the wide range of struggles against multiple forms of dispossession,[34] which in recent times have been classified as socio-environmental struggles against all kinds of extractivism, and which our collective has understood as constellations of struggles for the common. This work has led us into an expanded understanding of the idea of "the common" with its dual meanings: 1) as a social relation and 2) as a critical category. In addition, our work was greatly enriched by the perspective of political ecology, primarily as it was developed by Mina Navarro, who broadened the purview of our collective research into the intimate dynamics of communitarian weavings, inviting us to take up concepts like "interdependence" and self-regulation.[35] In this way, as we have written in a collaborative essay:

> *The common is produced*, it is made by many through the generation and constant reproduction of a multiplicity of associations and weavings and through social relations of collaboration that continuously enable the production and enjoyment of a large quantity of common goods, be they material or immaterial. The goods that are often called 'common'—water, seeds,

---

[33] Jaime Martínez Luna's work on *comunalidad* describes it as being composed of these four types of activity. A *cargo* is a position of responsibility, such as overseeing some aspect of a community's infrastructure or development.—Ed.

[34] Navarro, *Luchas por lo común*.

[35] Mina Lorena Navarro Trujillo y Daniele Fini (coords.), *Despojo capitalista y luchas comunitarias en defensa de la vida en México. Claves desde la ecología política* (Puebla/México: ICSyH-BUAP, 2016).

forests, the water distribution systems of certain communities, urban self-managed spaces, etc.—could not exist without the social relations that produce them. In fact, they cannot be understood without the people, organizing practices, processes of collective signification, affective ties, relations of interdependence and reciprocity that shape them every day, that produce these goods as common.

The production of the common, in our understanding, has a critical valance, given that:

Although [the multiple and diverse forms of producing the common] ambiguously and contradictorily coexist with capitalist social relations, they are not produced—or are minimally produced—within the capitalist sphere of value production.

They are produced and reinforced generally *against and beyond* capitalist social relations, enabling the very capacity for the development of struggles, given that we will only be able to generate concrete wealth if we are able to produce bonds that are not mediated—or not fully mediated—by capitalist relations.

In most cases, the social relations that produce the common often emerge as a result of the concrete and cooperative work of self-organized human communities; communities that create joint strategies to tackle common problems and needs and thus guarantee the reproduction and nurturing of the material and spiritual sustenance of their communities. In this sense, we argue that *the common is above all a social relation*, a social relation of association and cooperation that is *capable of enabling on a daily basis the social production and enjoyment of concrete wealth* as use values; that is, as material and immaterial goods that are necessary for the defense and satisfactory reproduction of life.[36]

Understanding the common in this way also led us to broaden the notion of the communitarian beyond ethnicity or inheritance, to define it as struggle, *making*, and collective creation. In particular, Mina Navarro has explored both the fragility and the power of *making the common in cities*.[37] We reiterate that we have no intention of disregarding the richness of the lessons that the resolute and determined struggles of Andean and Mesoamerican Indigenous peoples have offered us; rather, we understand the common as a specifically human—and therefore collective and individual—capacity to cultivate bonds for the satisfaction of *needs*, to weave networks based on reciprocal obligation, and to commit to the production of agreements for the use and management of what is collectively created.[38] Furthermore, we came to understand everyday caretaking and the deployment of this *capacity of form* as a key element and unifying thread in our understanding of social transformation as a systematic subversion of the existing order, which can regenerate collective bonds capable of sustaining the reproduction of life, against and beyond the colonial and patriarchal order of capital and the state.[39]

Having arrived at this partial synthesis of our work, we are finding new avenues and angles for exploration. The

[36] Gutiérrez, Navarro, y Linsalata, "Producing the Common."

[37] Navarro, "Una perspectiva socioecológica."

[38] Amaia Pérez Orozco, *Subversión feminista de la economía. Aportes para un debate sobre el conflicto capital-vida* (Madrid: Traficantes de sueños, 2014).

[39] Bolívar Echeverría, *Las ilusiones de la modernidad* (México: El Equilibrista/UNAM, 1995); Bolívar Echeverría, *Valor de uso y utopía* (México: Siglo XXI, 1998).

first is the need to subject to criticism the image of "revolution" inherited from the eighteenth century, as it emerged from the subjectivity defined by the romantic *ethos*, as an illusion of total rupture with a past to be demolished and a will to re-create society from scratch.[40] This notion, though perhaps diluted or disfigured, has accompanied leftist thought up to the present day. We have paid careful attention to the ever-present tension between the preservation of inherited and cultivated material and symbolic wealth and the transformation of forms of political appropriation, as well as the regeneration of and care for that material wealth. This has been a path for us to explore the meanings of social transformation generated by and held within struggles that illuminate horizons of rupture, which break with everything that denies the possibility of producing the common, while reclaiming the will to preserve and care for everything that sustains it.[41]

On this topic, our approach also dialogues with work on communality [*comunalidad*], which describes a "communal paradox" or a balance between conservation and creation. The critical nature of our approach—which understands communal creation as affirming and negating, rather than as mere difference—contributes to the conversation about what is shared by specific, historical experiences of those groups of people fighting to "continue to be what they are, while at the same time moving away from where the dominant order places them," to paraphrase Francisco López Bárcenas' wonderful description of the struggles of Indigenous peoples.

---

[40] Echeverría, *Las ilusiones de la modernidad.*

[41] Diego Castro, "Cierre del ciclo progresista en Uruguay y América Latina. Balance para relanzar horizontes emancipatorios," a paper presented at conference of the Latin American Studies Association (LASA), Lima, 2017.

The second offshoot we are nurturing—and which several of us are currently pursuing—also has a dual nature. We have taken on the challenge of reflecting on the common with an eye on sexual difference, dealing with the fundamental socio-natural fact that we exist as human beings who inhabit bodies that are diversely sexed, while keeping in play the far-reaching historical and social fact of patriarchal domination that repeatedly establishes and replicates a variety of odious differences and hierarchies between sexed bodies.[42] Drawing on contributions from the feminism of the 1960s, we came to understand that patriarchy operates by repeatedly converting difference into hierarchy. In this way, the patriarchal logic of continual and radical hierarchization of any difference is intimately intertwined with the crushing logic of capitalism. As well, the contributions of the Bolivian group Mujeres Creando, who, through the writings of María Galindo, describe the complex way in which the patriarchal pact is woven into colonial countries, have been crucial for us.[43] We distance ourselves from a liberal feminism that advocates for equality, while avoiding an uncritical notion of complementarity between sexed bodies, which is often used to conceal hierarchies, differentiated inclusions, and an array of oppressions and forms of violence, as it denies the distinctly patriarchal traits that structure and organize contemporary societies, both rural and urban, Indigenous and national.[44]

---

[42] Raquel Gutiérrez Aguilar, F. Escárzaga, J. Carrillo, E. Capece, y Borries Nehe (coords.), *Movimiento indígena en América Latina: resistencia y proyecto alternativo*, vol. III (México: UAM-BUAP-CIESAS-CEAM, 2014).

[43] María Galindo, *¡A despatriarcar! Feminismo urgente* (Buenos Aires: Ediciones Mujeres Creando/Lavaca, 2016).

[44] Tzul, *Sistemas de Gobierno Comunitario Indígena*.

With an attention to these ideas and incorporating arguments from political ecology, one of our current tasks is to explore the sexed characteristics of *making the common*, guided by the concept of *forms of interdependence*.[45] We understand that social relations based on commodity exchange, as developed by capitalist colonialism—which is not only a mode of production but above all a way of *organizing the natural world*[46] and thus the diverse bodies that compose it—are just *one way* of organizing the relations of interdependence that shape social life. When expropriation and continual exploitation of labor and its creations, as well as *multiple dispossessions* of collectively produced and shared social wealth are the central axis of economic activity, scarcity and precarity result.

A central piece of the historical process of the expansion of mercantile-capitalist relations in colonial contexts is the centering of the masculine experience of domination, which organizes the continuous exploitation and dominion over feminized bodies and colonized territories.[47] From the perspective of interdependence, we explored the *chain of separations*,[48] which have been historically imposed in at least three arenas. First, the separation between society and nature and the subsequent exploitation of the land and its resources, which is based on the mediation of a splintered, objectifying, steadily privatized, and disciplinary form of knowledge known as science. The second is the separation

---

[45] Navarro y Fini, *Despojo capitalista y luchas comunitarias en defensa de la vida en México.*

[46] Jason Moore, *Capitalism in the Web of Life: Ecology and the Accumulation of Capital* (London and New York: Verso, 2015).

[47] Silvia Federici, *La revolución feminista inacabada. Mujeres, reproducción social y lucha por lo común* (México: Escuela Calpulli, 2013); Galindo, *¡A despatriarcar! Feminismo urgente.*

[48] Navarro, "Una perspectiva socioecológica."

of the dispossessed from their means of existence[49] and their subsequent exploitation as formally-free workers, based on the mediation of the wage and, more broadly, money. The third is the separation of women from men and the subsequent appropriation—rendered invisible and almost automatic—of a significant part of their work for the reproduction of capital. Capital imposes a *patriarchal mediation* as a foundation for other social relations and as the institutional edifice that stabilizes and makes them endure.

With this concept of *patriarchal mediation*, we strive to name and shine a light on the feminine experience—and the experience of feminized bodies—of separation and blockage (obstruction, negation, disregard, distortion, rupture) of relations *between women as mediated by their own common and shared words.* While the specific form of lived patriarchal mediation shaping the experiences of woman and those inhabiting feminized bodies is always specific, particular and dependent on the location, we also believe that is communicable: it can be shared and understood through words that name what is lived and known, opening to conversation and the generation and regeneration of fruitful and creative bonds.

In this way, the study of both the separations organized by the aforementioned mediations of dominant knowledges, money and wages, and patriarchy—and especially the various ways in which these separations are undermined and challenged, evaded and overcome—is currently our central concern. The human capacity to create and regenerate bonds is, therefore, the essential aspect—both in theory and practice—of our collective work. We will briefly sum-

---

[49] Massimo De Angelis, "Marx y la acumulación primitiva: el carácter continuo de los 'cercamientos' capitalistas," *Theomai* #26 (julio–diciembre, 2012), https://www.redalyc.org/articulo. oa?id=12426097003.

marize then the core of our current endeavor in the form of a hypothesis.

The third analytic: the production of the common, by way of hypothesis

The production of the common—which always takes place as an activity within a weaving of interdependence—entails, above all else, the cultivation, revitalization, regeneration, and reconstruction of everything needed to guarantee collective life, against and beyond the separations and negations imposed by the logic of patriarchal capitalist dispossession and exploitation, as reinforced by the liberal state and its political forms.

We understand a communitarian weaving to be a specific and sexed collective subjectivity in motion, capable of itself producing reinvigorated forms of interdependence with the ability to generate concrete wealth. This weaving persists reflexively and critically to ensure: 1) the material and symbolic reproduction of collective life, 2) the durability and the balancing of the bonds it produces, while acknowledging sexual difference as well.

This is why communitarian weavings are never something simply given or inherited; instead, they are dynamic and diverse collective creations. They are repeated attempts at producing stable bonds, capable of providing and maintaining, adjusting and balancing, forms of self-regulation that sustain their existence over time.

We acknowledge that when studying such a wide array of practices and struggles, it may seem like our efforts are pointless or in vain. We believe this is not the case; rather, we strive to make careful distinctions in order to name as clearly as possible that which capital and its liberal political forms hide and dismiss. We experiment with reinvigorated syntactic forms that allow us to avoid the universalist tendency of the logic that structures Spanish, the colonial language we speak, a language that delimits and dictates what can and cannot be said. That's why we continually contest the deepest meanings of certain terms, transforming them and opening them to new connotations. With our entire bodies, we feel that our work is worthwhile as we must regenerate our sensate and intellectual capacities—currently disjointed and fragmented—to understand the world from the perspective of interdependence. To achieve this, what seems to us to be the most fruitful path is to both practice and to study *the common* as a social relation that is directly antagonistic to capital at multiple levels and scales.

BIBLIOGRAPHY

Almendra Quiguanas, Vilma Rocío. "Emancipación Nasa: luchas, contradicciones y desafíos. Cooptación, asimilación y captura para revertir el horizonte emancipatorio." Master's Thesis in Sociology, Puebla, ICSyH-BUAP, 2016.

Castro, Diego. "Cierre del ciclo progresista en Uruguay y América Latina. Balance para relanzar horizontes emancipatorios." Paper presented at the conference of the Latin American Studies Association (LASA), Lima, 2017.

De Angelis, Massimo. "Marx y la acumulación primitiva: el carácter continuo de los 'cercamientos' capitalistas." *Theomai* #26 (julio–diciembre 2012). https://www.redalyc.org/articulo.oa?id=12426097003.

Echeverría, Bolívar. *Las ilusiones de la modernidad.* México: El Equilibrista/UNAM, 1995.

Echeverría, Bolívar. *Valor de uso y utopía.* México: Siglo XXI, 1998.

Federici, Silvia. *Calibán y la bruja. Mujeres, cuerpo y acumulación originaria.* Buenos Aires: Tinta Limón, 2011.

Federici, Silvia. *Calibán y la bruja. Mujeres, cuerpo y acumulación originaria*. México: Pez en el Árbol/Tinta Limón, 2013.

Federici, Silvia. *La revolución feminista inacabada. Mujeres, reproducción social y lucha por lo común*. México: Escuela Calpulli, 2013.

Galindo, María. *¡A despatriarcar! Feminismo urgente*. Buenos Aires: Ediciones Mujeres Creando/Lavaca, 2016.

Gutiérrez Aguilar, Raquel. *¡A desordenar! Por una historia abierta de la lucha social*. México: Pez en el árbol, 2014.

Gutiérrez Aguilar, Raquel. "Amplifying feminist struggle in the wake of March 8." Translated by María José López. *Ojalá*, March 17, 2023. https://www.ojala.mx/en/ojala-en/amplifying-feminist-struggle-in-the-wake-of-march-8.

Gutiérrez Aguilar, Raquel. "Beyond the Arithmetic of Gender Equality." *Ojalá*, September 30, 2023.https://www.ojala.mx/en/ojala-en/beyond-the-arithmetic-of-gender-equality.

Gutiérrez Aguilar, Raquel. *Democratizaciones plebeyas*. La Paz: Colección Comuna, 2002.

Gutiérrez Aguilar, Raquel. *Desandar el laberinto. Introspección en la feminidad contemporánea*. México: Pez en el árbol, 2010.

Gutiérrez Aguilar, Raquel. "Forma comunal y forma liberal de la política." En *Pluriverso. Teoría política boliviana*. La Paz: Colección Comuna, Editorial Muela del Diablo, 2001.

Gutiérrez Aguilar, Raquel. *Horizonte comunitario-popular. Antagonismo y producción de lo común en América Latina*. México: Benemérita Universidad Autónoma de Puebla, 2015.

Gutiérrez Aguilar, Raquel. "Letters to my Younger Sisters." Translated by Dawn Marie Paley and Liz Mason-

Deese. *Ill Will*, February 8, 2023. https://illwill.com/letters-to-my-younger-sisters.

Gutiérrez Aguilar, Raquel. *Los ritmos del Pachakuti. Movilización y levantamiento indígena-popular en Bolivia (2000–2005)*. Buenos Aires: Tinta Limón/Universidad Internacional de Andalucía, 2008.

Gutiérrez Aguilar, Raquel. *Los ritmos del Pachakuti. Levantamiento y movilización en Bolivia (2000–2005)*. México DF: ICSyH-BUAP/Bajo Tierra Ediciones, 2009.

Gutiérrez Aguilar, Raquel. "Repensar lo político, pensar lo común. Claves para la discusión." En *Modernidades alternativas y nuevo sentido común: ¿hacia una modernidad no capitalista?* Coordinado por Lucía Linsalata, Daniel Inclán, y Márgara Millán. México: FCPyS-UNAM, 2016.

Gutiérrez Aguilar, Raquel. *Rhythms of the Pachakuti: Indigenous Uprising and State Power in Bolivia*. Translated by Stacey Alba D. Skar. Durham: Duke University Press, 2014.

Gutiérrez Aguilar, Raquel. "Social Reproduction, Rebellion and the Problem of the State." *Ojalá*, June 9, 2023. https://www.ojala.mx/en/ojala-en/reproduction-rebellion-and-the-problem-of-the-state.

Gutiérrez Aguilar, Raquel y Dawn Paley. "La transformación sustancial de la guerra y la violencia contra las mujeres en México." *Deportate, esuli, profughe. Rivista telemática di studi sulla memoria femminile* #30 (2016).

Gutiérrez Aguilar, Raquel y F. Escárzaga, J. Carrillo, E. Capece, y Borries Nehe (coords.). *Movimiento indígena en América Latina: resistencia y proyecto alternativo*, vol. III. México: UAM-BUAP-CIESAS-CEAM, 2014.

Gutiérrez Aguilar, Raquel y Huáscar Salazar Lohman. "Reproducción comunitaria de la vida. Pensando la transformación social en el presente." *el Apantle, Revista de Estudios Comunitarios, 'Común ¿para qué?'* #1. Puebla/ México: SOCEE, Octubre 2015.

Gutiérrez Aguilar, Raquel; Huáscar Salazar Lohman; y Gladys Tzul Tzul. "Leer el siglo XX a contrapelo. Constelaciones de historias comunitarias de luchas por territorios y autogobierno en Bolivia y Guatemala." *el Apantle, Revista de Estudios Comunitarios, '¿Común cómo? Lógicas y situaciones'* #2. Puebla/México: SOCEE, octubre 2016.

Gutiérrez Aguilar, Raquel, Mina Lorena Navarro, y Lucía Linsalata. "Producing the Common: Clues to Understand 'the Political.'" In *Social Sciences for an Other Politics: Women Theorising without Parachutes*. Edited by Ana Cecilia Dinerstein. Cham, Switzerland: Palgrave Macmillan, 2016.

Gutiérrez Aguilar, R., F. Escárzaga, J. Carrillo, E. Capece y Borries Nehe (coords.). *Movimiento indígena en América Latina: resistencia y proyecto alternativo*, vol. II. México: Casa Juan Pablos/CEAM/UAM/BUAP/UACM/GDF/ Diakonía/ CIDES/UMSA/UPEA, 2006.

Gutiérrez Aguilar, Raquel y Fabiola Escárzaga (coords.). *Movimiento indígena en América Latina: resistencia y proyecto alternativo*, vol. I. México: Casa Juan Pablos/ BUAP/UACM/UNAM/GDF, 2005.

Holloway, John. *Cambiar el mundo sin tomar el poder.* Puebla/México: ICSyH-BUAP/Bajo Tierra, 2010.

Holloway, John. *Agrietar el capitalismo: el hacer contra el trabajo*. Puebla/México: ICSyH-BUAP/Bajo Tierra, 2011.

Linsalata, Lucía y Huáscar Salazar Lohman (coords.). *Común ¿cómo y para qué?* Madrid: Traficantes de sueños, 2017.

Linsalata, Lucía (coord.). *Lo comunitario-popular en México: desafíos, tensiones y posibilidades*. Puebla/México: Instituto de Ciencias Sociales y Humanidades-BUAP, 2016.

Linsalata, Lucía. *Cuando manda la asamblea. Lo comunitario-popular en Bolivia: una mirada desde los sistemas
comunitarios de agua de Cochabamba.* La Paz: SOCEE/
Autodeterminación/Fundación, abril 2015.

Linsalata, Lucía. *El ethos comunal en la política boliviana.
Una aproximación a las formas comunales de la política
en el mundo aymara boliviano.* México: EAE Editorial,
2012.

Martínez Luna, Jaime. *Textos sobre el camino andado.*
Oaxaca: CSEIIO-CAMPO, 2013.

Méndez García, Elia. *De relámpagos y recuerdos . . . Minería
y tradición de lucha serrana por lo común.* Guadalajara:
Universidad de Guadalajara/CIESAS/Cátedra Jorge
Alonso, 2017.

Moore, Jason. *Capitalism in the Web of Life: Ecology and the
Accumulation of Capital.* London and New York: Verso,
2015.

Muraro, Luisa. "La independencia simbólica del poder."
Ponencia al Coloquio "Poder y política no son la misma
cosa" organizado por el Grupo Diótima, Universidad de
Verona, 10 de octubre de 2008.

Navarro Trujillo, Mina Lorena. "Una perspectiva
socioecológica para pensar el despojo múltiple y las
separaciones del capital sobre la vida." En *Naturaleza,
territorio y conflicto en la trama capitalista contemporánea*, 93–109. Compilado por Diego Pérez, Gonzalo
Barrios y Ezequiel Acsebrud. Buenos Aires: Extramuros
Ediciones/Theomai Libros, 2018.

Navarro Trujillo, Mina Lorena. *Hacer común contra la
fragmentación: experiencias de autonomía urbana.* Puebla/
México: Instituto de Ciencias Sociales y Humanidades-
BUAP, 2016.

Navarro Trujillo, Mina Lorena. *Luchas por lo común.
Antagonismo social contra el despojo capitalista de los
bienes naturales en México.* Puebla/México: Bajo Tierra/

Instituto de Ciencias Sociales y Humanidades-BUAP, 2015.

Navarro Trujillo, Mina Lorena, y Daniele Fini (coord.). *Despojo capitalista y luchas comunitarias en defensa de la vida en México. Claves desde la ecología política.* Puebla/México: ICSyH-BUAP, 2016.

Navarro Trujillo, Mina Lorena, y Claudia Composto (comp.). *Territorios en disputa. Despojo capitalista, luchas en defensa de los bienes comunes naturales y alternativas emancipatorias para América Latina.* México: Bajo Tierra Ediciones, 2014.

Negri, Antonio y Michael Hardt. *Commonwealth. El proyecto de una revolución del común.* Madrid: Akal, 2010.

Paley, Dawn. *Drug War Capitalism.* Oakland: AK Press, 2014.

Paley, Dawn. "La guerra en México a contrapelo: contrainsurgencia ampliada versus lo popular." *el Apantle: Revista de Estudios Comunitarios.* Puebla/México: SOCCEE/Pez en el árbol (octubre 2016): 181–197.

Pérez Orozco, Amaia. *Subversión feminista de la economía. Aportes para un debate sobre el conflicto capital-vida.* Madrid: Traficantes de sueños, 2014.

Reyes Díaz, Itandehui. "Los cercamientos de los cuerpos-territorios y la lucha contra el feminicidio en Ecatepec." Master's Thesis, Puebla, BUAP, 2017.

Tapia, Luis. *Política salvaje.* La Paz: Comuna/Muela del Diablo/Clacso, 2008.

Tischler, Sergio. *Memoria, tiempo y sujeto.* Guatemala: BUAP/F&G, 2005.

Tzul Tzul, Gladys. *Sistemas de gobierno comunitario indígena. Mujeres y tramas de parentesco en Chuimeq'ena'.* Guatemala: SOCEE/Tz'ikin, 2016.

Varela, Francisco J. *Conocer: Las ciencias cognitivas. Tendencias y perspectivas.* Barcelona: Editorial GEDISA, 1988.

Varela, Francisco J. y Humberto Maturana. *El árbol del conocimiento. Las bases biológicas del entendimiento humano.* Buenos Aires: Lumen, 1984.

ABOUT THE AUTHOR

Raquel Gutiérrez Aguilar (México DF, 1962) is an organizer who has participated in numerous struggles and uprisings in Latin America over the last four decades. From the civil wars in Central America in the 1980s to Indigenous uprisings in Bolivia, she has contributed to struggles both as an active participant and as a theorist of movement strategies, horizons, and possibilities.

After spending five years in prison in Bolivia, and energized by the Water War in Cochabamba, Gutiérrez Aguilar returned to México in 2001. Since then, she has experimented working with and alongside women in multiple ways: in autonomous organizations, social centers, publishing projects, the academy, and most recently, via journalism with the digital weekly *Ojala.mx*.

Gutiérrez Aguilar is the author of the following volumes, all of which draw on her life experiences: *¡A desordenar! Por una historia abierta de la lucha social* (1995), *Desandar el laberinto* (1999), and *Cartas a mis hermanas más jóvenes 1 y 2* (2020 and 2021), the first of which came out in English as *Letter to My Younger Sisters* (2023). She has also written about various struggles and political moments, for example:

The Rhythms of the Pachakuti (2014) and *Horizontes comunitarios-populares en América Latina* (2015).

Together with other comrades, she has compiled experiences and debates taking place among Indigenous and communitarian struggles in Latin America in a three-volume series titled *Movimiento indígena en América Latina: resitencia y transformación social* (2005, 2007, and 2011) as well in *Comunalidad, tramas comunitarias y producción de lo común: Debates contemporáneos desde América Latina* (2018).

ABOUT THE EDITOR

Brian Whitener is an Associate Professor of Romance Languages and Literatures at the University at Buffalo and author of *Crisis Cultures: The Rise of Finance in Mexico and Brazil* (University of Pittsburgh Press, 2019), *Face Down* (Timeless Infinite Light, 2016), and *The 90s* (speCt!, 2022). He is an editor on two forthcoming books: *Border Abolition Now* (Pluto Press, 2024) and *Abolir ya: otra justicia es posible* (Bajo Tierra, 2024). Other writing and translation projects include: *De gente común: Arte, política y rebeldía social*, edited with Lorena Méndez and Fernando Fuentes (Universidad Autónoma de la Ciudad de México, 2013) and the translations of *Grupo de Arte Callejero: Thoughts, Actions, Practices* (Common Notions, 2019) and *Genocide in the Neighborhood: State Violence, Popular Justice, and the 'Escrache'* (Common Notions, 2023).

ABOUT THE TRANSLATOR

JD Pluecker works with language; that is, a living thing, a thing of life and history. Their undisciplinary work inhabits the intersections of writing, history, translation, art, interpreting, bookmaking, queer/trans aesthetics, nonnormative poetics, language justice, and crossborder cultural production. They have translated numerous books from Spanish, including: *Gore Capitalism* (Semiotext(e), 2018); *Antígona González* (Les Figues Press, 2016); *Writing with Caca* by Luis Felipe Fabre (Green Lantern Press, 2021); and *Trash* by Sylvia Aguilar Zéleny (Deep Vellum Press, 2022). Their book of poetry and image, *Ford Over*, was released in 2016 from Noemi Press, and in 2019 Lawndale Art Center supported the publication of *The Unsettlements: Dad.* From 2010–2020, they worked as part of the transdisciplinary collaborative Antena Aire, and from 2015–2020 with the local social justice interpreting collective, Antena Houston. JD has exhibited work at Blaffer Art Museum, the Hammer Museum, Project Row Houses, and more. More info at jdpluecker.com and http://antenaantena.org.

ABOUT COMMON NOTIONS

Common Notions is a publishing house and programming platform that fosters new formulations of living autonomy. We aim to circulate timely reflections, clear critiques, and inspiring strategies that amplify movements for social justice.

Our publications trace a constellation of critical and visionary meditations on the organization of freedom. By any media necessary, we seek to nourish the imagination and generalize common notions about the creation of other worlds beyond state and capital. Inspired by various traditions of autonomism and liberation—in the US and internationally, historical and emerging from contemporary movements—our publications provide resources for a collective reading of struggles past, present, and to come.

Common Notions regularly collaborates with political collectives, militant authors, radical presses, and maverick designers around the world. Our political and aesthetic pursuits are dreamed and realized with Antumbra Designs.

www.commonnotions.org
info@commonnotions.org

BECOME A COMMON NOTIONS MONTHLY SUSTAINER

These are decisive times ripe with challenges and possibility, heartache, and beautiful inspiration. More than ever, we need timely reflections, clear critiques, and inspiring strategies that can help movements for social justice grow and transform society.

Help us amplify those words, deeds, and dreams that our liberation movements, and our worlds, so urgently need.

Movements are sustained by people like you, whose fugitive words, deeds, and dreams bend against the world of domination and exploitation.

For collective imagination, dedicated practices of love and study, and organized acts of freedom.
By any media necessary.
With your love and support.

Monthly sustainers start at $15.

commonnotions.org/sustain

MORE FROM
COMMON NOTIONS

Grupo de Arte Callejero: Thought, Practices, and Actions
Grupo de Arte Callejero
Translated by the Mareada Rosa Translation Collective

ISBN: 978-1-942173-10-6 (print)
ISBN: 978-1-942173-34-2 (eBook)
$22.00 | 6 x 9 | 352 pages
Subjects: Art/Latin America/Social Theory

An indispensable reflection on what was done and what remains to be done in the social fields of art and revolution.

Grupo de Arte Callejero: Thought, Practices, and Actions tells the profound story of social militancy and art in Argentina over the last two decades and propels it forward. For Grupo de Arte Callejero [Group of Street Artists], militancy and art blur together in the anonymous, collective, everyday spaces and rhythms of life. Thought, Practices, and Actions offers an indispensable reflection on what was done and what remains to be done in the social fields of art and revolution.

Every new utopian struggle that emerges must to some extent be organized on the knowledge of its precedents. From this perspective, Grupo de Arte Callejero situates their experience in a network of previous and subsequent practices that based more on popular knowledge than on great theories. Their work does not elaborate a dogma or a model to follow, but humbly expresses their interventions within Latin American autonomous politics as a form of concrete, tangible support so that knowledge can be generalized and politicized by a society in movement.

Without a doubt this will not be the most exhaustive book that can be written on the GAC, nor the most complete, nor the most acute and critical, but it is the one GAC wanted to write for themselves.

MORE FROM
COMMON NOTIONS

19 and 20: Notes for a New Insurrection
Colectivo Situaciones
With Contributions by Marcello Tarì, Liz
Mason-Deese, Antonio Negri, and Michael
Hardt
Translated by Nate Holdren and Sebastian
Touza

ISBN: 978-1-942173-48-9 (print)
ISBN: 978-1-942173-62-5 (eBook)
$20.00 | 6 x 9 | 288 pages
Subjects: Latin America/Insurrections/
Resistance

From a rebellion against neoliberalism's miserable failures, notes for a new insurrection and a new society.

19 and 20 tells the story of one of the most popular uprisings against neoliberalism: on December 19th and 20th, 2001, amidst a financial crisis that tanked the economy, ordinary people in Argentina took to the streets shouting "¡Qué se vayan todos!" (They all must go!) Thousands of people went to their windows banging pots and pans, neighbors organized themselves into hundreds of popular assemblies, workers took over streets and factories. In those exhilarating days, government after government fell as people invented a new economy and a new way of governing themselves.

It was a defining moment of the antiglobalization movement and Colectivo Situaciones was there, thinking and engaging in the struggle. Their writings during the insurrection have since been passed hand to hand and their practice of militant research modelled widely as a way of thinking together in a time of rebellion. Today, as a staggering debt crisis deepens, we see the embers from that time twenty years ago in the mutual aid initiatives and new forms of solidarity amidst widespread vulnerability.

Revisiting the forms of counterpower that emerged from the shadow of neoliberal rule, Colectivo Situaciones reminds us that our potential is collective and ungovernable.

MORE FROM
COMMON NOTIONS

Genocide in the Neighborhood:
State Violence, Popular Justice, and the
'Escrache'
Colectivo Situaciones
Edited and Translated by Brian Whitener

ISBN: 978-1-942173-86-1 (print)
ISBN: 978-1-945335-02-0 (eBook)
$20.00 | 5 x 8 | 160 pages
Subjects: Latin America/Insurrections/
Resistance

Another justice is possible. *Genocide in*
the Neighborhood **documents the theories,**
debates, successes, and failures of a rebellious tactic to build popular
power and transformative justice.

Genocide in the Neighborhood explores the autonomist practice of the
"escrache," a series of public shamings that emerged in the late 1990s to
honor the lives of those tens of thousands disappeared and exterminated
under the Argentinean military dictatorship (1976 to 1983) and to protest
the amnesty granted to perpetrators of state violence.

Through a series of hypotheses and two sets of interviews, Colectivo
Situaciones highlights the theories, debates, successes, and failures of the
escraches—those direct and decentralized ways to agitate for justice that
Brian Whitener defines as "something between a march, an action or happening, and a public shaming."

Genocide in the Neighborhood also follows the popular Argentine uprising
in 2001, a period of intense social unrest and political creativity that led
to the collapse of government after government. The power that ordinary
people developed for themselves in public space soon gave birth to a movement of neighborhoods organizing themselves into hundreds of popular
assemblies across the country, while the unemployed took over streets and
workers occupied factories. .

Printed in the USA
CPSIA information can be obtained
at www.ICGtesting.com
JSHW081349161024
71833JS00001B/6